85 LANDMARK SUPREME COURT JUDGMENTS

For UPSC Civil Services Prelims, Mains and Interview, State PCS, CLAT & Judiciary Exams

Dr. P.K. Agrawal, IAS (Retd.)
Ex-Jt. Secy. Ministry of Law & Justice, GoI

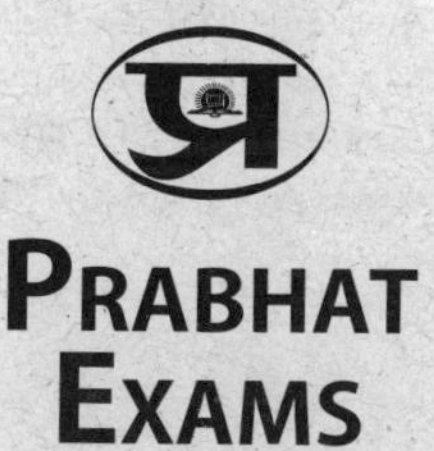

PRABHAT EXAMS

Publisher

PRABHAT EXAMS

An imprint of Prabhat Prakashan Pvt. Ltd.

4/19 Asaf Ali Road, New Delhi–110 002

Ph. 23289555 • 23289666 • 23289777 • Helpline/ 7827007777

e-mail: prabhatbooks@gmail.com • Website: www.prabhatexam.com

Edition
2025

Price
Five Hundred Rupees Only

ISBN 978-93-90906-64-2

Printed at
R-Tech Offset Printer, Delhi

85 LANDMARK SUPREME COURT JUDGMENTS
by Dr. P.K. Agrawal, IAS (Retd.)

ISBN 978-93-90906-64-2

₹ 500.00

Introduction

"The law reigns supreme". In a country like India, this statement is surely a well acknowledged truth. It is upon the ground norms laid down by the Constitution that the edifice of Indian Democracy is built. Hence to understand the soul of India, it is important to understand the Constitution of India. However, the Indian Constitution, unlike any other piece of document is a 'living document'. The different parts and provisions of Constitution have been interpreted by the Supreme Court of India in several of its Landmark Judgements. The law laid down by the Supreme Court in its judgement is the law of the country. The Supreme Court has the final say on the text or the provision of the Constitution. Supreme Court is the final arbiter of law of India. Sometimes the law through subsequent ruling of the Supreme Court is changed but it has already left an imprint. Such list of cases is also given in the end. Therefore in order to deepen the understanding of the Constitution, it becomes pertinent to develop knowledge of such judgements. Also, as a part of an informed citizenry and as prospective bureaucrats, judges and lawyers everyone should build awareness about the cases which have helped to shape the Indian judicial system and the interpretation of Indian Constitution as we know it today. According to Dr. B.R. AMBEDKAR, *"Constitution is not a mere lawyers' document, it is a vehicle of life and its spirit is always the spirit of age"*.

Supreme Court has made it dynamic by its ever changing decisions. An attempt has been made in this treatise to present those judgements to which even of some High Courts which have changed the direction of thinking, action and delivery of justice in the country and have laid down guidelines for the future India. It is just possible that some of the judgements have been missed out of plethora of judgements of the Apex Court, High Courts or various Tribunals. However, it was with an eye to make this book more useful for the civil services aspirants of the UPSC and other State Public Service Commissions.

Inspite, I am sure that the book will be welcomed by all.

– Dr P.K. AGRAWAL

An overview of the Constitution of India

Constitution is the supreme law of our country and contains the fundamental law of the land. It is also called the "Suprema-Lex" or the paramount law of the country. All the three organs of the Indian state, i.e. executive, legislative and judiciary derive their powers from the Constitution. Every legislative enactment in the country has to conform to the Constitution. All statutes, laws, bylaws, orders and rules derive their power from Constitution only. And hence they all have to function within the limits prescribed by it otherwise they shall be termed unconstitutional and therefore null and void.

The Constitution of India came into power on 26th January, 1950. At the hour of its reception, the Constitution contained 395 Articles and the Eight Schedule and was around 145,000 words long, making it the longest public Constitution to ever be embraced. Each Article within the Constitution was formulated by the individuals from the Constituent Assembly, who sat for 11 meetings and 166 days to stipulate the Constitution, over a time of two years and 11 months.

Indian Constitution is the longest in the world. It originally contained 395 Articles in 22 parts and 8 schedules and it came into force on 26th January, 1950.

At present, the Constitution of India has 448 Articles in 25 parts and 12 schedules. 104 amendments have been made in the Indian Constitution till January 25, 2020.

It was framed By the Constituent Assembly. The Constituent Assembly of India was elected to write the Constitution of India. After India's independence, this Assembly also served as the nation's first Parliament.

Given below are some important facts about the Constituent Assembly of India:

- Type-Unicameral
- History:
    (1) Founded on 9 December 1946
    (2) Disbanded on 24 January 1950
    (3) Preceded by Imperial Legislative Council
    (4) Succeeded by Parliament of India
- Temporary Chairman- Sachchidananda Sinha, INC
- President- Dr. Rajendra Prasad, INC
- Chairman of the Drafting Committee- Dr. B. R. Ambedkar, SCF
- Vice Presidents- Harendra Coomar Mookerjee, T. Krishnamachari
- Structure
  Seats-389 (Dec. 1946-June 1947); 299 (June 1947-Jan. 1950)
- Political groups
  INC: 208 seats
  AIML: 73 seats
  Others: 15 seats
  Princely States: 93 seats

Elections

Voting system- Single Transferable Vote

The Indian Constitution was derived from multiple sources. However, its primary source is the Government of India Act of 1935 from which it borrowed features like federal scheme, office of Governor, judiciary etc.

The Constitution of India provides for a parliamentary form of government both at the centre and state level. This form of government is also called the Westminster Model of Government. Under this form of government, the members of the parliament are directly elected by the people. The President is the Constitutional head and the real executive and legislative powers rest with the council of ministers whose head is the Prime Minister. Such Council of Ministers is collectively responsible to Lok Sabha. Hence this form of government is also called the responsible form of government.

Contents

Preamble of the Indian Constitution

WE, THE PEOPLE OF INDIA, having solemnly resolved to constitute India into a 1[SOVEREIGN SOCIALIST SECULAR DEMOCRATIC REPUBLIC] and to secure to all its citizens: JUSTICE, social, economic and political; LIBERTY of thought, expression, belief, faith and worship; EQUALITY of status and of opportunity; and to promote among them all FRATERNITY assuring the dignity of the individual and the 2 [unity and integrity of the Nation]; IN OUR CONSTITUENT ASSEMBLY this twenty sixth day of November, 1949, do HEREBY ADOPT, ENACT AND GIVE TO OURSELVES THIS CONSTITUTION.

The Constitution begins with the Preamble. The Preamble states the subjects, aims, and objective of the Constitution. It has also been called as key to the minds of the Constitution makers.

The Preamble is based on the 'Objective Resolution' drafted and moved by Jawaharlal Nehru and adopted by the Constituent Assembly. The 42nd Amendment Act, 1976 inserted three new words in the Preamble-Socialist, Secular, and Integrity.

It consists of important terms like secular, socialist etc. They are discussed in detail below-

(a) **Sovereign:** This word shows independence of India from outside authorities and that it is no more a Dominion but an independent country.

(b) **Socialist:** It points to the welfare state that India is which aims to provide social justice to its citizens.

(c) **Secular:** The word 'secular' implies that there is no specific religion of the State. People are free to practise any religion and all religions shall be respected. The State does not provide priority to any religion.

(d) **Democracy:** It has been popularly defined as the government of the people, for the people and by the people. Indian democracy is indirect, representative democracy where people elect their representatives who take the legislative and executive decisions on their behalf.

(e) **Republic:** The government in a republic is elected by free and fair elections and the ultimate power lies in the hands of the citizens.

(f) **Justice:** Justice in the Preamble means social, economic, and political justice.

(g) **Liberty:** Liberty is a stage where there is absence of restrictions. It is the power to do what is allowed by the law of the land.

(h) **Equality:** It means providing equal rights to all citizens without any discrimination.

(i) **Fraternity:** It means a sense of brotherhood and a sense of unity among the citizens of the country, irrespective of caste, creed or religion.

Is Preamble a part of the Constitution?

In the *Berubari Union Case of 1960* it was held that the Preamble isn't a part of Constitution. However, in the *Keshavanand Bharti Case of 1973,* SC declined the view and held that the Preamble was a part of the Constitution. Hence the Preamble is to be read as a part of the Indian Constitution and therefore its principles are justiciable in the court or law and fall under the purview of judicial review.

Part I: The Union and its Territory

Part 1 of the Constitution of India consists of Articles 1-4. According to Article 1(3), the territory of India shall comprise of:

(a) States' territories

(b) Union territories

(c) Other territories that may be acquired by means of treaty, succession and conquests.

Article 2

Parliament may by law admit into the Union, or establish, new States on such terms and conditions as it thinks fit.

This Article gives power to the parliament to admit any new state into the union; and to form a new state. This Article was applied by the court in the case of *R.C. Poudyal vs Union* of India to admit the State of Sikkim into Union of India.

1

R.C. Poudyal vs Union of India
AIR 1993 SC 1804
A.L. Sikkim was admitted as a State in the Union of India

Facts: In 1950, Sikkim became a protectorate state of India. This meant that Indian government was responsible only for the defence, communication and external affairs of Sikkim. Sikkim was ruled by the monarchs of Chogyal dynasty. In the late 1960s and early 70s, the dynasty faced popular agitation for the demands of conducting of elections. Bowing down to the pressure, the monarch agreed to hold the elections. The new elected government of Sikkim passed a resolution in its Assembly for the merger with the Union of India. In pursuance of this resolution, the Indian Parliament passed the 36th Amendment Act for the merger of state with the union of India. This Amendment Act was challenged in the Supreme Court.

Decision: The court upheld the Amendment Act under Article 2 of the Constitution. The Article gave power to Parliament to admit new states into the Union on the terms and conditions it deemed fit. However, the court also remarked that the exercise of power under Article 2 by the Parliament falls under the purview of judicial review. Hence the Central Government could not exercise it at its whims and fancies.

Article 3 of the Constitution

Parliament may by law—

(a) form a new State by separation of territory from any State or by uniting two or more States or parts of States or by uniting any territory to a part of any State;

(b) increase the area of any State;

(c) diminish the area of any State;

(d) alter the boundaries of any State;

(e) alter the name of any State.

Provided that no Bill for the purpose shall be introduced in either House of Parliament except on the recommendation of the President and unless, where the proposal contained in the Bill affects the area, boundaries or name of any of the States 1***, the Bill has been referred by the President to the Legislature of that State for expressing its views thereon within such period as may be specified in the reference or within such further period as the President may allow and the period so specified or allowed has expired.

Explanation I.—In this Article, in clauses (a) to (e), "State'' includes a Union territory, but in the proviso, "State'' does not include a Union territory.

Explanation II—The power conferred on the Parliament by clause (a) includes the power to form a new State or Union territory by uniting a part of any State or Union territory to any other State or Union territory.

It gives the Parliament power to draw and redraw the political map of the country. Using this Article, the parliament can form new states by: separating any territory from a state; by uniting any territory with any state; or by uniting territories of any two or more states. Under Article 3, Parliament can also increase or diminish the area and alter the boundary or name of any state.

On prima facie reading of Articles 2 and 3, it becomes apparent that while on the one hand Article 2 deals with the establishment and admission of new states into union of India, on the other hand Article 3 deals with reorganization of the already existing states of Union of India.

It was in the case of 'In re. Berubari Union' where the question, 'whether Article 3 gives Parliament power to cede the territory of Union of India to a foreign country?' came up before the Supreme Court.

2

In re. Berubari Union and Exchange of Enclaves
AIR 1960 SC 845
To cede a territory from India, amendment of the Constitution is required

Facts: The case pertains to the exchange of enclaves between India and Pakistan. As per the exchange, Berubari Enclave was to be transferred to Pakistan and Cooch Bihar Enclaves were to come to India. While the opposition in Parliament demanded an amendment act to be passed to bring the transfer of territory into effect, the then Government insisted in the court that Article 3 accorded power on the state to transfer the territory of the union to a foreign state. The transfer deal led to huge public outcry and hence the President of India sought the opinion of Supreme Court under Article 143 over the issue.

Decision: The Court observed that under Article 3 the area separated from a state needs to be added to a state within the territory of India only. Such an area cannot be ceded to a foreign state or a country. In order to bring into effect the agreement relating to exchange of territories an amendment under Article 368 is required.

Part II: Citizenship

Part 2 of the Constitution which consists of Articles 5-11 is named 'Citizenship'.

The question that now arises is *what is meant by citizenship*?

In technical terms, Citizenship is the status of an individual perceived under the custom or law of a sovereign state as an individual from or having a place with the state. Each state is allowed to decide the conditions under which it will perceive people as its residents, and the conditions under which that status will be pulled back.

The Constitution of India defines its population in three different categories:

(a) Persons.

(b) Citizens.

(c) Minorities.

The segregation of the population in these different categories is important because the Indian Constitution accords different rights to different category of citizens, i.e., not every fundamental right provided under the Constitution is available to everyone.

For example, equality before law under Article 14 is available to all persons, whether citizen or not, whereas right against discrimination under Article 15 is available only to citizens of India. Cultural and educational rights under Article 29 is available only to Minorities in the country.

Citizenship in India is further categorized in two:

A. Citizenship given by the Constitution

B. Citizenship given by the Citizenship Act of 1955.

Category A, i.e., Citizenship given by the Constitution, deals with Citizenship given at the commencement of the Constitution, i.e., on 26th January 1950. The law regarding the same is given under Part 2 of the Constitution under Articles 5-11.

Category B, i.e., Citizenship given by the Citizenship Act of 1955, deals with Citizenship given after the commencement of the Constitution. The Act which deals with the acquisition and loss of citizenship of India has been amended in the years 1986, 1992, 2003, 2005 and 2019.

The scope of discussion of this book is limited to the citizenship given under category A, i.e., Citizenship given by the Constitution.

According to Part 2, Articles 5-11 of the Constitution, the following categories of persons were declared to be Indian citizens on the date of commencement of the Constitution:

(a) Persons who were domiciled in India.

(b) Persons who had migrated to India from Pakistan.

(c) Persons who had migrated to Pakistan but had returned to India under permanent settlement before the commencement of Constitution.

(d) Persons living abroad but subsequently registered as citizens of India at an Indian consulate.

Part III: Fundamental Rights

Part 3 of the Constitution which consists of Articles 12-35 is named 'Fundamental Rights'.

It is the most important part of the Indian Constitution as it deals with civil rights and liberties in India. It also contains the provisions that provide for remedy in case of violation of such rights and liberties.

The Fundamental Rights given under Part III are different from other ordinary rights in respect that they cannot be taken away by the legislature through an ordinary legislation. Any amendment to the Fundamental Rights requires a Constitutional Amendment. In the case of *Maneka Gandhi vs Union of India (1978),* Justice Bhagwati stated fundamental rights to be fundamental to the full intellectual, moral and spiritual attainment of an individual in his/her life. In *M. Nagraj vs Union of India (2006),* the Supreme Court held the object behind inclusion of Fundamental Rights in Constitution is to establish rule of law.

DEVELOPMENT OF FUNDAMENTAL RIGHTS:

AROUND THE WORLD

- **Magna Carta in 1215:** Released in 13th century feudal England, Magna Carta for the first time provided civil liberties such as protection against unlawful arrests and excessive fines.

- **Bill of Rights in 1689:** Passed by British Parliament, it widened the scope of civil liberties provided in Magna Carta.
- **Declaration of Rights of Man and Citizen in 1789:** Proclaimed in 18th century France, it declared certain rights to be sacred to man.
- **Bill of Rights in 1791:** America incorporated Bill of Rights in its Constitution in the year 1791.

IN INDIA

- **Swaraj Bill of 1895:** Declared certain rights to be inviolable and fundamental such as right to freedom of expression and equality before law.
- India Home Rule Bill in 1924.
- Nehru Committee in 1928.
- Resolution on Fundamental Rights in Congress' Karachi session of March 1931.
- Coming into force of Indian Constitution on 26th January, 1950. The Part 3 of Indian Constitution containing Fundamental Rights is known as Magna Carta of Indian democracy.

CLASSIFICATION OF FUNDAMENTAL RIGHTS

Fundamental Rights under Part III are further classified in six different types. They are as follows-

- Right to Equality– Articles 14 to 18.
- Right to Freedom– Articles 19 to 22.
- Right Against Exploitation– Articles 23 and 24.
- Right to Freedom of Religion– Articles 25 to 28.
- Right to Cultural and Educational Minorities– Articles 29 and 30.
- Right to Constitutional Remedies– Article 32.

Article 12

In this Part, unless the context otherwise requires, "the State" includes the Government and Parliament of India and the Government and the Legislature of each of the States and all local or other authorities within the territory of India or under the control of the Government of India.

According to Article 12, the term 'State', for the purpose of Part 3 and Part 4 of the Constitution[1] shall include the following-

(1) Executive of Union and State, i.e., Union government and State government respectively.

(2) Legislature of Union and Sate, i.e., Parliament and State Legislature respectively.

(3) All local and other authorities within the territory of India or under the control of the government of India.

As far as the above mentioned three categories are concerned, the first two (No. 1 & 2) are unambiguously defined. The term 'Local Authority' used under Article 12(3) is defined in section 3(31) of the General Clauses Act, 1897. Local Authority includes local self-governing bodies such as Panchayat, Municipal Committee etc. It is only for the term 'other authority' under Article 12(3) where the ambiguity lies. Supreme Court in several of its landmark judgements has made interpretation of the term 'other authorities'.

In the case *University of Madras vs Shantabai (1954),* the court held for an authority to be called state under Article 12, like government, it too must wield sovereign power. In the case of *Ujjam Bai vs State of U.P. (1962)*, Court overruled the judgment of *University of Madras vs Shantabai* and held that for an authority to be called state under Article 12, need not wield sovereign power like Government.

In the case of *Rajasthan State Electricity Board vs Mohanlal (1967),* the Apex Court ruled that the term 'other authorities' includes every statutory body that has power to affect fundamental rights. It is not necessary that such body shall have powers of a sovereign.

In *Sukhdev vs Bhagatram (1975),* to answer the question whether an authority would be called state under Article 12 or not the court devised a test which it named 'test of functionality'. The court only had to ascertain the function performed by such authority. If the function performed was an important 'public

[1]Definition of state given under Article 12 is only applicable to Parts III and IV of the Constitution.

function', close to the government function, then such an authority would be called state under Article 12.

In the cases of *R.D. Shetty vs International Airport Authority (1979)* and *Ajay Hasia vs Khalid Mujib (1981)*, the court devised another test called 'control test'. As per this test, the court was only to look at-

(a) whether the state owned the majority share capital in that authority;

(b) is it heavily dependent upon state finances;

(c) whether it enjoys monopoly status;

(d) is there a deep state control;

(e) whether it performed an important public function. With regard to an authority if the answer to any of the above questions is 'yes' then such an authority is to be termed state under Article 12.

Both the 'control test' and 'functionality test' were held to be complementary to each other and hence were read together in the case of *Som Prakash Rekhi vs Union of India (1981)*.

In *Pradeep Kumar vs Indian Institute of Chemical Biology (2002),* the court overruled both the control test and functionality test. It held that for a body to be called 'state', it must be financially, functionally, and administratively dominated by the government. The court applied the test laid down in Pradeep Kumar in its landmark judgement in the case of *BCCI vs Cricket Association of Bihar (2015)* to hold that BCCI is not state under Article 12.

Article 13

(1) All laws in force in the territory of India immediately before the commencement of this Constitution, in so far as they are inconsistent with the provisions of this Part, shall, to the extent of such inconsistency, be void.

(2) The State shall not make any law which takes away or abridges the rights conferred by this Part and any law made in contravention of this clause shall, to the extent of the contravention, be void.

(3) In this Article, unless the context otherwise requires:-

(a) "law" includes any ordinance, order, bye-law, rule, regulation, notification, custom or usage having in the territory of India the force of law;

(b) "laws in force" includes laws passed or made by a Legislature or other competent authority in the territory of India before the commencement of this Constitution and not previously repealed, notwithstanding that any such law or any part thereof may not be then in operation either at all or in particular areas.

(4) Nothing in this Article shall apply to any amendment of this Constitution made under Article 368.

According to this Article, any law which is in derogation of the fundamental rights given under Part 3 of the Constitution is unconstitutional and hence void.

Article 13(1) talks about the Constitutionality of pre Constitutional laws and declares them to be '*void to the extent to which they are inconsistent with Part Three of the Constitution.*' The principles behind Article 13(1) are of the Doctrine of Eclipse and Doctrine of Severability.

What is the Doctrine of Eclipse?

This doctrine is applied only on pre-constitutional laws. According to this doctrine if any law which was valid at its inception but became void due to repugnancy with Part III of the Constitution (fundamental rights) then such law is to be treated dormant, not dead. The dormant law shall become valid when the repugnancy in it is removed by subsequent amendment/s, made either to the law or to Part III of the Constitution itself, e.g., in the case of *Bhikaji Narain Dhankaras vs State of M.P*, the Motor Vehicle Act of 1947 which allowed for state monopoly in the motor vehicle business was held to be repugnant to Article 19 (1) (g) of the Constitution. However, after the first Constitution Amendment Act of 1951 (in which sub clause 1 to clause 6 of Article 19 was added), government monopoly in certain businesses was allowed. By the virtue of this amendment the Motor Vehicle Act of 1947 was held to have again become valid.

Article 13(2) deals with post Constitutional laws. It states that the state shall not make such laws that take away a citizen's fundamental rights granted to him/her by part three of the Constitution. Laws which contravene those rights should be held unconstitutional to the extent of contravention. This principle is derived from the Doctrine of Severability.

What is the Doctrine of Severability?

It is applicable on both pre and post-constitutional laws. According to this, only such portion of any law is to be held invalid which is repugnant to Part III of the Constitution. The rest of the statute is to be held valid. Both Articles 13(1) and 13(2) enshrine the principles of this doctrine. The major question about the application of the doctrine of severability is what would be the impact of the severance of the unconstitutional part of statute on its Constitutional part. This question was answered by the Supreme Court in the case of *A.K. Gopalan vs State of Madras (1950)*. In this case, the court held that in order to determine whether the Constitutional part can be severed from the unconstitutional part or not, the intention of the legislature should be taken into consideration. Hence, 'the intention of legislature was held to be the determining factor'. And to determine the intention of legislature, the text, object, preamble, history etc. of the statute shall be considered.

Article 13(3) gives definition of the term 'law' and 'law in force' for the purpose of part three of the Constitution.

Whether an amendment to the Constitution under Article 368 is law under the definition given by Article 13(3)?

While on the one hand Article 13 puts limitation on the law making and amending power of the legislature by subjecting every law to part three of the Constitution, Article 368 on the other hand gives Parliament power to amend the Constitution. Therefore arises the question that whether an amendment made to the Constitution under Article 368 is law under the definition given by Article 13(3) and hence subject to limitation imposed by Part three of the Constitution or whether the Constitution amending power of the parliament unlimited. This question was first raised before the Supreme Court in the case of *Shankari Prasad vs U.O.I. (1951)*.

3

Board of Control for Cricket in India vs Cricket Association of Bihar

AIR 2015 SC 3194 = 2015(3)SCC251

BCCI is amenable to Writ Jurisdiction

Decision: The majority view favours the view that BCCI is amenable to the writ jurisdiction of the High Court under Article 226 even when it is not 'State' within the meaning of Article 12. The rationale underlying that view if we may say with utmost respect lies in the "nature of duties and functions" which the BCCI performs. It is common ground that the respondent-Board has a complete sway over the game of cricket in this country. It regulates and controls the game to the exclusion of all others. It formulates rules, regulations, norms and standards covering all aspect of the game. It enjoys the power of choosing the members of the national team and the umpires. It exercises the power of disqualifying players which may at times put an end to the sporting career of a person. It spends crores of rupees on building and maintaining infrastructure like stadia, running of cricket academies and supporting State Associations. It frames pension schemes and incurs expenditure on coaches, trainers etc. It sells broadcast and telecast rights and collects admission fee to venues where the matches are played. All these activities are undertaken with the tacit concurrence of the State Government and the Government of India who are not only fully aware but supportive of the activities of the Board. The State has not chosen to bring any law or taken any other step that would either deprive or dilute the Board's monopoly in the field of cricket. On the contrary, the Government of India have allowed the Board to select the national team which is then recognized by all concerned and applauded by the entire nation including at times by the highest of the dignitaries when they win tournaments and bring laurels home. Those distinguishing themselves in the international arena are conferred highest civilian awards like the Bharat Ratna, Padma Vibhushan, Padma Bhushan and Padma Shri apart from sporting awards instituted by the Government. Such is the passion for this game in this country that cricketers are seen as icons by youngsters, middle-aged and the old alike. Any organization or entity that has such pervasive control over the game and its affairs and such powers as can make dreams end up in smoke or come true cannot be said to be undertaking any private activity. The functions of the Board are clearly public functions, which, till such time the State intervenes to takeover the same, remain in the nature of public functions, no matter discharged by a society registered under the Registration of Societies Act. Suffice it to say that if the Government not only allows an autonomous/private body to discharge functions which it could in law takeover or regulate but even lends its assistance to such a non-government body to undertake such functions which by their very nature are public functions, it cannot be said that the functions are not public functions or that the entity discharging the same is not answerable on the standards generally applicable to judicial review of State action. Our answer to question No.1, therefore, is in the negative, qua, the first part and affirmative qua the second BCCI may not be State under Article 12 of the Constitution but is certainly amenable to writ jurisdiction under Article 226 of the Constitution of India.

Shankari Prasad vs U.O.I., AIR, 1951 SC 458

Constitutional Amendment is not law.

Facts: In this case, the first Constitutional Amendment Act was challenged in Supreme Court. This Constitutional Amendment Act was known for the abolition of the zamindari system. In this Constitutional Amendment Act, Articles 31A and 31B were inserted in the Constitution which curtailed the then fundamental right to property up to a great extent.

Decision: The Supreme Court in this case held that word 'law' under Article 13 does not include a Constitutional amendment passed by Parliament and hence the fundamental right against the Constitutional amendment cannot be claimed.

The judgment of Shankari Prasad case was reiterated by the court in the case of Sajjan Singh vs State of Rajasthan.

5

I.C. Golak Nath vs State of Punjab

AIR 1967 SC 1643

Parliament can not amend fundamental rights.

Facts: The Golaknath family owned 500 acres of land. However due to promulgation of land tenure act by state of Punjab, the family was required to give up a major portion of their land to the Government. Hence, the family challenged the Land Tenure Act in the court. It was argued that under Article 19 of the Constitution they had fundamental right to property which was violated by the abovementioned Act.

The question raised before the Supreme Court was regarding the extent of the Parliament's amending power.

Decision: The judgment was given by a bench of 11 judges. In this case, the court observed that the Parliament's amendment power was not unlimited but limited. Power under Article 368 was held to be subject to limitation given under Article 13. Therefore, the court held that the Parliament cannot amend the fundamental rights given under the Part III of the Constitution.

After the Golaknath case verdict, a threatened Parliament, in order to establish its supremacy over the judiciary, brought the 24th Constitutional Amendment Act under which Article 13(4) was added to Constitution which made the Constitution amending power of the Parliament under Article 368 absolute. Hence, it can be said that the Golaknath case's verdict was reversed by the 24th Constitution Amendment Act.

6

Kesavananda Bharati vs State of Kerala

AIR 1973 SC 1461

Basic structure of the Constitution can not be amended by Parliament

The Supreme Court laid down the idea of Basic Structure during this case. According to this theory, a number of the provisions of the Constitution of India form its basic structure which aren't amendable by Parliament by exercise of its constituent power under Article 368.

Facts of the case: In 1970, Swami Kesavananda Bharati, head of a Hindu Matha situated in Kerala challenged the Kerala Land Reforms Act of 1963 which the then government by the 29th Constitution Amendment Act had put under the 9th Schedule of the Constitution to prevent it from any kind of judicial review. The petitioner challenged the Constitutional validity of 29th Constitutional Amendment Act. Union of India, which was made party to the suit contended that Parliament's power to amend the Constitution was unlimited. The hearings for the case lasted for five months. The bench of 13 Supreme Court judges that decided the case is the largest bench in the history of independent India for any case. The case was continuously heard for 68 days and arguments inter alia were adduced by the known legal luminary Nani Palkhivala, Senior Advocate that Parliament has no power to make any law which amends the basic features of the Constitution of India. The ratio of the bench was 7:6. i.e., 7 judges gave assent while 6 judges dissented. It was the view of the majority (i.e., 7 judges) which became the final verdict in this case.

This was the case where the validity of the 24th, 25th and 29th amendments made to the Constitution of India were put before the Supreme Court. The main question was associated with the character, extent and scope of amending power of the Parliament under the Constitution.

Decision:

The key observations made in this case were as follows:

(1) The case of I.C. Golak Nath v. State of Punjab, in which the court had held that the fundamental rights given under the Constitution could not be amended by the Parliament was overruled.

(2) The 24th Constitution Amendment Act of 1971 which gave Parliament the power to amend any part of the Constitution was upheld.

(3) Amendments made by Article 368 were held to be valid. Although the parliament wasn't given the power to change the Basic Structure or the essential framework of the Constitution; The court although, didn't specify precisely the elements of Basic Structure in an exhaustive manner. However some judges gave a couple of examples.

(4) The amendment of Article 368(4) which took away court's power to review the Constitution was declared invalid and unconstitutional.

(5) The amendment of Article 31C containing the words "and no law containing a declaration that it's for giving effect to such policy shall be called in question in any court on the ground that it doesn't give effect to such policy" was held to be invalid.

Basic Structure: The origin of the concept of basic structure is found in the German Constitution. In India, the Basic Structure doctrine as propounded in the case of Kesavananda Bharati declared certain parts and features of the Constitution to be so important to its spirit that they are beyond the Parliament's Constitution amending power. However, the court in its judgement purposely refrained from giving any exhaustive definition of the concept of Basic Structure. The reason being that the court wanted to keep the transformative nature of Indian Constitution alive instead of making it rigid and stuck in time.

In the Kesavananda Bharati judgement, the court pronounced certain parts to form the Basic Structure of Indian Constitution. They were as follows-supremacy of the Constitution, the republican and democratic form of Government, separation of powers, the secular and federal character of the Constitution, unity and integrity of the nation, Preamble, sovereign democratic republican nature of the Constitution, social, economic and political justice, liberty of thought, expression, belief, faith and worship, and the equality of status and opportunity.

In future judgments, the Court added several other features to this list.

Comments: This case represents the essence of Indian thought. It postulated a basic concept that since it is the people of India who framed the Constitution for this country at the Constituent Assembly convened for this purpose, it should be only such Constituent Assembly which is empowered either to amend the basic features of the Constitution or frame a new Constitution. The present Parliament has no power to amend the basic features. What are the basic features of the Constitution may be spelt out subsequently as and when such issues came up before the Court. Till now, several judgments of the Supreme Court have held that Parliamentary system of the Government, separation of powers between the executive, judiciary and lagislature, the separation of powers between and among the States and Centre even as the system being unitary, the electoral method are basic featurs. The fundamental rights are also basic features. Such of the amendments only which promote basic features are welcome but not those which aim at abridging the rights arising out of basic features. Accordingly this judgment stands out as an inspiring point for interpreting the Constitution of India in future.

7

Indira Gandhi vs Raj Narain

AIR 1975 SC 2299

Election of Mrs Indira Gandhi was held void

Facts: One of Indira Gandhi's political adversary Raj Narain challenged her election to her constituency to be void due to corrupt practices undertaken by her. Allahabad High Court adjudged in favour of Raj Narain and held Mrs. Gandhi's election to be void under Representation of People's Act. Soon after this judgment the Parliament passed the thirty ninth amendment act which added case clause 4 to Article 329A. Clause 4 had put the election of P.M and speaker under Schedule IX of the Constitution and hence out of judiciary's power to review any irregularity in the same. The constitutionality of this amendment act was challenged in the Supreme Court.

Decision: Supreme Court held clause 4 of Article 329A to be violative of the principle of 'Rule of Law' which the court defined as protection against the arbitrary exercise of power by the executive. The court in this case also held 'Rule of Law' and 'free and fair election' to be parts of Basic Structure of Constitution.

8

Minerva Mills vs Union of India AIR 1980 SC 1789

Parliament cannot have unfettered power of amendment of the Constitution

In this case, the concept of Judicial Review and Limited Amending Powers of Parliament were held to be part of Basic Structure of the Constitution. Minerva Mills was the last case in which Judiciary had to reassert its supremacy over Parliament with respect to interpretation of the Constitution.

Facts: In this case, the 42nd Constitutional Amendment Act passed in 1976, i.e., during the emergency years was challenged in the Supreme Court. Under this Amendment Act, two clauses were added to Article 368 that had the effect of suppressing Judiciary's control over the interpretation of Constitution. One of the amended clauses stated that no Constitutional amendment made by Parliament could be called in question before any court of law in the country. The second clause gave the Parliament unfettered powers to amend the Constitution. It stated that there would be no limitation over the Constitution amending power of the Parliament.

Decision: The judgment in this case was given by a five-judge bench which held the amendments made to Article 368 were unconstitutional. The clauses added to Article were hence struck down. The court also held Judicial Review and Limited Amending Powers of Parliament to be part of Basic Structure of the Constitution.

Right to Equality

Article 14 to 18 form part of group of rights titled 'Right to Equality.'

Article 14

The State shall not deny to any person equality before the law or the equal protection of the laws within the territory of India.

It provides to 'all persons': (a) Equality before law (b) Equal protection of law

Equality before law means that equals should be treated alike. Every legislative decision shall be made keeping in mind the principle of equality before law. Hence it prohibits class legislation. Equal protection of law means that every law shall be similarly applied on similarly placed people. Its application is mostly in the domain of executive actions. The aim of both these principles is to provide equal justice to all.

Article 14 prohibits making any law that discriminates between two individuals. However, it also mandates treating only equals alike. The Supreme Court in the case of *Budhan Chaudhary vs State of Bihar* held that although Article 14 prohibits classification for the purpose of making law but it does not prohibit 'reasonable classification.' Article 14 does not stop the legislature from making beneficial laws for a section of society which has been historically oppressed as long as such law reasonably classifies such people into a distinct category.

9

State of Bombay vs F.N. Balsara (1951)

Classification under Article 14 should be reasonable

In this case the court held that to pass the test of 'reasonable classification' following two conditions shall be fulfilled:

(1) The classification must be based on an 'intelligible differentia'. The term 'intelligible differentia' means an intelligent reason for the statute to classify and differentiate people into such groups.

(2) There shall be a 'Rational Nexus' between the classification and object sought to be achieved by the statute.

The Reasonable Classification test was over the years realized to be limiting the scope of judicial review of legislative action. State could now state any objective and make any arbitrary classification and justify it on the basis of such objective. This lacuna in the 'Reasonable Classification' test was however remedied in the judgment of E.P. Royappa vs State of Tamil Nadu.

10

E.P. Royappa vs State of Tamil Nadu (1974)

State action cannot be arbitrary

Reversing the doctrine of Reasonable Classification given in the case of F.N. Balsara, the S.C. formed a new doctrine. In this case the court held that concept of equality is a dynamic concept, hence it cannot be cribbed, confined or cabined within the traditional limits. In this judgement, the court coined a new doctrine of anti-arbitrariness/reasonableness. The three-judge bench in this case opined that an arbitrary action (both legislative and executive is antithetical to both Constitutionality and logic. It also violates the principle of equality enshrined in Article 14. It went on further to define an arbitrary action to be an action which is not based on rational grounds; is ill thought; or is done with a malafide intention. Hence according to this doctrine, the objective of Article 14 is to eliminate arbitrariness from the state's action.

Article 15

(1) The State shall not discriminate against any citizen on grounds only of religion, race, caste, sex, place of birth or any of them.

(2) No citizen shall, on grounds only of religion, race, caste, sex, place of birth or any of them, be subject to any disability, liability, restriction or condition with regard to—

(a) Access to shops, public restaurants, hotels and places of public entertainment; or

(b) The use of wells, tanks, bathing ghats, roads and places of public resort maintained wholly or partly out of State funds or dedicated to the use of the general public.

(3) Nothing in this Article shall prevent the State from making any special provision for women and children.

(4) Nothing in this Article or in clause (2) of Article 29 shall prevent the State from making any special provision for the advancement of any socially and educationally backward classes of citizens or for the Scheduled Castes and the Scheduled Tribes.

(5) Nothing in this Article or in sub-clause (g) of clause (1) of Article 19 shall prevent the State from making any special provision, by law, for the advancement of any socially and educationally backward classes of citizens or for the Scheduled Castes or the Scheduled Tribes in so far as such special provisions relate to their admission to educational institutions including private educational institutions, whether aided or unaided by the State, other than the minority educational institutions referred to in clause (1) of Article 30.

It provides for prohibition of discrimination. According to Article 15(1), the state shall not discriminate against any citizen 'only' on the grounds of religion, race, caste, sex, and place of birth. However, if any other relevant factor is added to any of the above grounds, then it provides for valid discrimination. Article 15 is an application of the principle of equality enshrined in Article 14. It prohibits discrimination only on certain grounds while Article 14 prohibits discrimination on all grounds.

11

State of Madras vs Champakam Dorairajan
AIR 1951 SC 226
Reservation on the basis of Caste is not permissible

Facts: It was in the year 1921 that the then State Government of Madras province, on the demand of one Justice Party had passed an order providing for reservation of government jobs for non-Brahmins in the state government. It was called the Communal GO. Later, its scope was expanded to provide for reservation in government colleges too. It was in the year 1951, even before the first general elections were conducted, that Dorairajan, an aspiring medical student filed a petition in the Madras High Court challenging the Communal G.O. on the basis that it violated the fundamental right of equality given under Article 15. The High Court held that the law discriminates on the basis of caste and hence declared it unconstitutional. It also made the observation that unlike Article 16(4) which specifically authorizes the state to make reservations for backward classes in government jobs, there is no such provision under Article 15.

An appeal against the High Court decision was made in the Supreme Court in March 1951. The argument made before the Supreme Court by the state of Madras in the favour of reservation provisions that it gave effect to Article 46 which was a Directive Principle of State Policy.

Issue before S.C.: Are reservation provisions for admission to college Constitutionally valid?

Decision: Supreme Court in this case upheld the High Court's decision which declared the law to be Constitutionally invalid. Doing a strict reading of the Article 15, the Supreme Court read the word 'only' in Article 15 to prohibit reservation only on the basis of caste. The court also observed that it violates the right guaranteed under Article 29(2) of the Constitution.

The decision led to widespread protests all across the state of Madras. It forced the parliament to pass an amendment to the Constitution. Article 15(4) was added. It provided state with power to make special provisions for any 'Socially and Educationally Backward Classes', notwithstanding anything contained in Article 15 and Article 29 (2).

M.R. Balaji vs State of Mysore 1963 AIR SC 649

Reservation should not exceed 50% of the total seats

In 1962, the state of Mysore followed a reservation policy where 62% seats in engineering and medical colleges were reserved for the students of SC, ST, and OBC category. This policy was challenged in the Supreme Court on the grounds of Constitutionality. The court, keeping in the mind the varied interests involved in this case such as rewarding merit and upliftment of backward classes gave a very balanced decision. It upheld the practice of reservation for students of backward classes on the grounds of Article 15(4) and 16(4), however, it also set a limit to such reservation. It affirmed that in no case reservation shall exceed 50% of the total seats, otherwise it would be an assault on the meritorious candidates. It also held that caste should not be the sole criterion of an affirmative action for the simple reason that except for Hindus, members of other communities do not recognize caste-based distinction.

13

Indira Sawhney vs Union of India AIR 1993 SC 477

Reservation to OBC is permissible.

Facts: The seeds of this case were sown long back in 1953 when the First Backward Classes Commission was formed. Its chairman was Kaka Kalelkar. It identified more than 2000 backward classes in India and recommended reservation as way of their social upliftment. Its recommendations were never implemented. Over two decades later, the then Prime Minster Morarji Desai fulfilled his electoral promise and constituted second such backward classes commission in 1979. It was set up under the chairmanship of B.P. Mandal, former Chief Minister of Bihar. In 1980, the commission submitted its report. It applied three broad parameters- social, educational, and economic to ascertain which of the classes could be termed socially and educationally backward. According to its report, OBCs constituted 52% of country's total population. Since 23% reservation already existed for SCs and STs, it recommended 27% reservation for OBCs in order to not breach the 50% reservation limit imposed by the court in the Balaji Case. In 1990, the VP Singh government decided to implement the recommendations of the Mandal Commission. It led to widespread protests and agitations. The government issued orders to implement the recommendations of the Mandal Commission. Apart from the reservations for OBSs, the order also provided 10% reservations for other economically backward sections who were not covered by the other reservation schemes. The matter was challenged in the Supreme Court.

Issue: Constitutionality of the government order extending reservations to OBCs and EWS.

Decision: A nine judge bench was constituted to hear the matter. The majority judgment was pronounced by six judges while other three dissented. The court upheld the extension of reservation to OBSs to be Constitutionally valid under Articles 15(4) and 16(4). However, in its decision it directed that the benefit of reservation shall not be extended to those who formed part of creamy layer, i.e., a section whose family income was above the prescribed limit. It held the second part of the order which extended the benefits of the reservation to the EWS to be unconstitutional. It observed that Constitution did not provide for reservation based solely on the economic grounds as the purpose of the reservation is not poverty eradication but the social upliftment of backward classes. It also recognized the 50% reservation limit set in the Balaji case. It disallowed the Mandal Commission recommendation of extending reservation to promotions in jobs too. However, within three years of this judgment the Parliament amended the Constitution and added Article 16(4A) to extend reservation in promotions to SCs and STs.

Article 16

(1) There shall be equality of opportunity for all citizens in matters relating to employment or appointment to any office under the State.

(2) No citizen shall, on grounds only of religion, race, caste, sex, descent, place of birth, residence or any of them, be ineligible for, or discriminated against in respect of, any employment or office under the State.

(3) Nothing in this Article shall prevent Parliament from making any law prescribing, in regard to a class or classes of employment or appointment to an office 1[under the Government of, or any local or other authority within, a State or Union territory, any requirement as to residence within that State or Union territory] prior to such employment or appointment.

(4) Nothing in this Article shall prevent the State from making any provision for the reservation of appointments or posts

in favour of any backward class of citizens which, in the opinion of the State, is not adequately represented in the services under the State.

2[(4A) Nothing in this Article shall prevent the State from making any provision for reservation 3[in matters of promotion, with consequential seniority, to any class] or classes of posts in the services under the State in favor of the Scheduled Castes and the Scheduled Tribes which, in the opinion of the State, are not adequately represented in the services under the State].

4[(4B) Nothing in this Article shall prevent the State from considering any unfilled vacancies of a year which are reserved for being filled up in that year in accordance with any provision for reservation made under clause (4) or clause (4A) as a separate class of vacancies to be filled up in any succeeding year or years and such class of vacancies shall not be considered together with the vacancies of the year in which they are being filled up for determining the ceiling of fifty per cent reservation on the total number of vacancies of that year].

(5) Nothing in this Article shall affect the operation of any law which provides that the incumbent of an office in connection with the affairs of any religious or denominational institution or any member of the governing body thereof shall be a person professing a particular religion or belonging to a particular denomination.

This Article deals with right to equality in matters of public employment. Article 16(1) lays down the general rule equality of opportunity to all citizens in matters pertaining to employment with the state. Article 16(2) lays down the specific rule that state shall not discriminate between citizens in matters pertaining to employment only on the grounds of race, caste, descent, and place of birth, sex, residence or any of them. Article 16(3), 16(4), and 16(5) that follow lay down exception to the rule of equality as enumerated under Articles 16(1) and 16(2).

14

State of Kerala vs N.M. Thomas (1976) 2 SCC 310

Relaxation to the OBC candidates is permissible.

Facts: Government of Kerala had passed order requiring all the lower division clerks (LDCs) in the state to qualify an exam in order to be promoted to Upper division clerks (UDCs). However, it had also provided certain relaxation to the candidates belonging to the backward classes. The order was challenged in the court on the ground that it violated the principle of Equality enshrined in Article 16(1) and is not covered by Article 16(4).

Issue: Whether the differential treatment is constitutionally valid?

Decision: The court observed that the differential treatment meted to the candidates of the backward classes fulfils the test of reasonable classification (as discussed earlier in this chapter) and also has a rational nexus to the object sought to be achieved by the state, i.e., providing equal opportunity to the historically disadvantaged people.

It held that the order is covered by Article 16(4) and did not violate equality of opportunity given under Article 16(1) as law provides for treating only likes alike. In its decision, the court upheld egalitarianism over equality. Egalitarianism is the principle of providing differential treatment to the disadvantaged so that they can compete with the rest. The then chief justice Ray in this case held that Article 16(4) is not an exception to 16(1) but is a method of achieving goals of equality enshrined in Article 16(1). This judgment gave rise to the group subordination principle according to which the prime goal of Article 16 is to achieve equality between groups and not between individuals.

15

Ram Singh vs Union of India, (2015) 4 SCC 697

Jat Reservation is not permissible.

Facts: In 1997, in response to numerous petitions, the National Commission for Backward Classes ["NCBC"] carried out a study, at the end of which it recommended the inclusion of Jats in the Central List only for two districts of Rajasthan. Subsequently, in response to numerous representations to review this decision, the NCBC decided to approach the Indian Council of Social Science Research (ICSSR), asking them to conduct a survey in various states (UP, Haryana, Madhya Pradesh, Rajasthan, Himachal Pradesh and Gujarat), in order to determine the socio-economic status of Jats. By a subsequent Cabinet decision, the states of Bihar, Uttarakhand and NCT of Delhi were also referred to the NCBC. The ICSSR submitted a report (but made no specific recommendations about inclusion/exclusion in the Central List). The report was discussed by the NCBC, which also held public hearings. The NCBC submitted a report to the government, stating that "*the Jat Community had not fulfilled the criteria for inclusion in the Central List of OBCs.*" But on 02.03.2014, the cabinet rejected this report, on the ground that it did not take into account "*ground realities.*" Two days later, via a notification, Jats were placed in the Central List for the nine states.

Decision: The Supreme Court overturned a government decision to grant reservations to the Jat community in nine states (by including them in the Central List of Backward Classes "Central List". The Supreme Court held that though caste may be a prominent and distinguishing factor for easy determination of backwardness, social groups who would be most deserving must necessarily be a matter of continuous evolution. The court also added that new practices, methods and yardsticks have to be continuously evolved, moving away from caste-centric definition of backwardness. Additionally, the government's contention that Jats were on the State Lists of eight out of the nine states was rejected by the Court, on the ground that those lists were made more than a decade ago, and that "*a decision as grave and important as involved in the present case which impacts the rights of many under Articles 14 and 16 of the Constitution must be taken on the basis of contemporaneous inputs and not outdated and antiquated data.*" The Court also found that the minutes of the Cabinet meeting held just before the Notification reflected a focus on the educational "backwardness" of the Jat community by highlighting school, college and graduate enrolment. The "backwardness" contemplated under Article 16, however, was social backwardness. Consequently, the Court held that the cabinet notification ignored relevant material (the NCBC report) and, in turn, based itself upon irrelevant material (educational parameters and decade-old data).

16

Ashoka Kumar Thakur vs Union of India and Others (2008)

6 SCC 1 = Creamy layer principle does not apply to STs and SCs.

Facts: Constitution 93rd Amendment Act, 2005 and Central Educational Institutions (Reservation in Admissions) Act 5 of 2007 were the subject matter of this case in which several points as regards reservation in posts in Government service and seats in educational institutions were reaffirmed. The question specifically raised and finally decided with emphasis is about the applicability of creamy layer. The Court held that the creamy layer exclusion does not apply to STs and SCs. The reasoning of the Court is contained in paras 184, 185 and 186 at pages 511 to 513 as follows:

"So far, the Court has not applied to "creamy layer" principle to the general principle of equality for the purpose of reservation. The "creamy layer" so far has been applied only to identify the backward class, as it required certain parameters to determine the backward classes. "Creamy layer" principle is one of the parameters to identify backward classes. Therefore, principally, the "creamy layer" principle cannot be applied to STs and SCs, as SCs and STS are separate classes by themselves. Ray, C.J., in an earlier decision, stated that "Scheduled Castes and Scheduled Tribes are not a caste within the ordinary meaning of caste". And they are so identified by virtue of the notification issued by the President of India under Articles 341 and 342 of the Constitution. The President may, after consultation with the Governor, by public notification, specify the castes, races or tribes or parts of or groups within castes, races or tribes which for the purpose of the Constitution shall be deemed to be Scheduled Castes or Scheduled

Tribes. Once the notification is issued, they are deemed to be the members of Scheduled Castes or Scheduled Tribes, whichever is applicable. In *E.V. Chinnaiah v. State of A.P.*, concurring with the majority judgment, S.B. Sinha, J. said:

"The Scheduled Castes and Scheduled Tribes occupy a special place in our Constitution. The President of India is the sole repository of the power to specify the castes, races or tribes or parts or groups within castes, races or tribes which shall for the purposes of the Constitution be deemed to be Scheduled Castes. The Constitution (Scheduled Castes) Order, 1950 made in terms of Article 341(1) is exhaustive. The object of Articles 341 and 342 to provide for grant of protection to the backward class of citizens who are specified in the Scheduled Castes Order and Scheduled Tribes Order having regard to the economic and education backwardness wherefrom they suffer. Any legislation which would bring them out of the purview thereof or tinker with the order issued by the President of India would be unconstitutional.

A plea was raised by the respondent State that categorisation of Scheduled Castes could be justified by applying the "creamy layer" test as used in *Indra Sawhney vs. Union of India*, which was specifically rejected in para 96 of *E.V. Chinnaiah case*. It is observed:

"96. But we must state that whenever such a situation arises in respect of Scheduled Caste, it will be Parliament alone to take the necessary legislative steps in terms of Clause (2) of Article 341 of the Constitution. The States concededly do not have the legislative competence therefor."

Moreover, right from the beginning, the Scheduled Castes and Scheduled Tribes were treated as a separate category and nobody ever disputed indeitification of such classes. So long as "creamy layer" is not applied as one of the principles of equality, it cannot be applied to the Scheduled Castes and Scheduled Tribes. So far, it is applied only to identify the osically and educationally backward classes. We make it clear that for the purpose of reservation, the principles of "creamy layer" are not applicable for Scheduled Castes and Scheduled Tribes."

Comment: This judgment as a matter of fact contains the summary of all important cases so far delivered on the subject of reservations.

Article 17

"Untouchability" is abolished and its practice in any form is forbidden. The enforcement of any disability arising out of "Untouchability" shall be an offence punishable in accordance with law.

Article 17 abolishes and forbids practice of untouchability in any form. It further declares that the enforcement of any disability arising out of untouchability shall be an offence punishable in accordance with law. It is Article 35 of the Constitution that gives Parliament the power to make any law penalizing the act of untouchability. Using this power, the Parliament enacted the Protection of Civil Rights Act, 1955 and Schedule Caste Schedule Tribe Prevention of Atrocities Act, 1989.

Article 18

(1) No title, not being a military or academic distinction, shall be conferred by the State.

(2) No citizen of India shall accept any title from any foreign State.

(3) No person who is not a citizen of India shall, while he holds any office of profit or trust under the State, accept without the consent of the President any title from any foreign State.

(4) No person holding any office of profit or trust under the State shall, without the consent of the President, accept any present, emolument, or office of any kind from or under any foreign State. Provides for abolition of titles conferred on a person such as Sir, Maharaja etc. However, titles conferred by state, military titles and academic titles are exempt from operation of Article 18.

Articles 19 to 22 are often read together under the heading 'right to freedom.' They together form the most important part of the Constitution. Different parts of this Article deals with different types of freedom.

Article 19

(1) All citizens shall have the right—

(a) to freedom of speech and expression;

(b) to assemble peaceably and without arms;

(c) to form associations or unions;

(d) to move freely throughout the territory of India;

(e) to reside and settle in any part of the territory of India; 1[and]

2 * * * * *

(g) To practise any profession, or to carry on any occupation, trade or business.

(2) Nothing in sub-clause (a) of clause (1) shall affect the operation of any existing law, or prevent the State from making any law, in so far as such law imposes reasonable restrictions on the exercise of [the right conferred by the said sub-clause in the interests of the sovereignty and integrity of India,] the security of the State, friendly relations with foreign States, public order, decency or morality, or in relation to contempt of court, defamation or incitement to an offence.

(3) Nothing in sub-clause (b) of the said clause shall affect the operation of any existing law in so far as it imposes, or prevent the State from making any law imposing, in the interests of 4[the sovereignty and integrity of India or] public order, reasonable restrictions on the exercise of the right conferred by the said sub-clause.

(4) Nothing in sub-clause (c) of the said clause shall affect the operation of any existing law in so far as it imposes, or prevent the State from making any law imposing, in the interests of the sovereignty and integrity of India or public order or morality, reasonable restrictions on the exercise of the right conferred by the said sub-clause.

(5) Nothing in sub-clauses (d) and (e) of the said clause shall affect the operation of any existing law in so far as it imposes, or prevent the State from making any law imposing, reasonable restrictions on the exercise of any of

the rights conferred by the said sub-clauses either in the interests of the general public or for the protection of the interests of any Scheduled Tribe.

(6) Nothing in sub-clause (g) of the said clause shall affect the operation of any existing law in so far as it imposes, or prevent the State from making any law imposing, in the interests of the general public, reasonable restrictions on the exercise of the right conferred by the said sub-clause, and, in particular, 2[nothing in the said sub-clause shall affect the operation of any existing law in so far as it relates to, or prevent the State from making any law relating to,—

(i) the professional or technical qualifications necessary for practising any profession or carrying on any occupation, trade or business; or

(ii) the carrying on by the State, or by a corporation owned or controlled by the State, of any trade, business, industry or service, whether to the exclusion, complete or partial, of citizens or otherwise].

It talks about six fundamental freedoms which the Constitution guarantees to the citizens and the restrictions that are attached to those freedoms. Article 19(1) enumerates those six freedoms whereas Articles 19(2) to 19(6)mention the restrictions to which those six freedoms are subject to. It is to be noted here that restrictions on the freedoms can be imposed only through a law passed by legislature and such restrictions should be reasonable in nature. Following are the six fundamental freedoms provided under Article 19:

(a) Freedom of speech and expression
(b) Freedom to assembly peaceably and without arms
(c) Freedom to form associations or unions
(d) Freedom to move freely throughout the territory of India
(e) Freedom to reside and settle in any part of the territory of India; and
(f) Freedom to practice any profession or to carry any trade or occupation

17

Amit Sahni vs Commissioner of Police & Ors.

Civil Appeal No. 3282/2020/07-10-2020

In Shaheen Bagh, reasonable restriction to hold protest can be imposed.

Facts:

- In Delhi's Shaheen Bagh, women led peaceful protests were organised from 15 December 2019 till the advent of COVID-19, i.e., March 2020, to oppose the enactment of the Citizenship Amendment Act, 2019 (CAA). The CAA removes the 'illegal immigrant' status of Hindus, Sikhs, Buddhists, Jains, Parsis and Christians who arrived in India before 31 December 2014 from Afghanistan, Bangladesh or Pakistan, excluding only the Muslim community. As a result, Muslim women gathered in Shaheen Bagh to demand the revocation of the CAA.
- The grievance made in the petition was that the persons opposing the Citizenship Amendment Act and the National Register of Citizens, the details of which were yet to be propounded, had adopted a method of protest which resulted in the closure of the Kalindi Kunj-Shaheen Bagh stretch, including the Okhla underpass from 15.12.2019. It was submitted that the public roads could not be permitted to be encroached upon in this manner and, thus, a direction be issued to clear the same.

Decision:

- The Court held that the Shaheen Bagh protestors do have a right to protest and express dissent under Articles 19(1)(a) and 19(1)(b) which grant the right to free speech and the right to peaceful assembly, respectively. However, the

Court highlighted that these rights are subject to reasonable restrictions pertaining to the sovereignty of the State and public order.

- Relying on its decision in Mazdoor Kisan Shakti Sangathan vs. Union of India, the Court said that the rights of the protestors have to be balanced with the rights of the commuters. It therefore, gave an order to the Delhi Administration to act in "their responsibility" to ensure that public spaces and roads are not occupied by the protestors, indefinitely. It further held that this limitation also applied to protests which had sought prior permission from administrative authorities, such as the Shaheen Bagh protests.
- A reasonable restriction in the form of seeking prior permission of the authorities to hold the protest at a designated time and place can be imposed. However, in doing so, the Court said that authorities should not have discretionary powers in granting permission to the protestors.

18

Shreya Singhal vs Union of India AIR 2015 SC 1523

Section 66A of IT Act, 2000 is void restricting freedom of speech and expression.

This case deals with the Freedom of Speech and Expression provided under Article 19 (1) (a) and the restrictions with regard to the same given under Article 19(2). Article 19(2) mentions certain grounds such as security of the state and public order on which restrictions on the Freedom of Speech and Expression provided under Article 19 (1) (a) can be made however it is also necessary that such restrictions shall be reasonable in nature.

Facts: In this case, the Constitutionality of Section 66A of the IT Act, 2000 was challenged in the Supreme Court. The section made making certain kinds of statements made on the internet punishable with jail. It was alleged in several petitions made before the Supreme Court that the section violated freedom of speech and expression provided under Article 19 (1) (a) as the restrictions given under it are not reasonable as per the standards prescribed by Article 19(2). It was argued that the section is arbitrary and vague as it does not mention any valid definition of making what kind of statements would be punishable. It left room for arbitrary exercise of power by the executive to gag free speech.

Issue: Does Section 66A of the IT Act, 2000 violate Article 19 (1) (a)?

Decision: Supreme Court upheld the arguments of the petitioner and declared Section 66A IT ACT, 2000 to be unconstitutional. Public order is mentioned as one of the grounds of restricting free speech under Article 19 (2). In this case, the court enunciated the 'test of clear and present danger.' According to this test, until and unless a speech does not pose a real and eminent danger to public order it shall not be censored or restricted. Applying this test, the court held that Section 66A IT ACT, 2000 does not lay down a clear ground for restricting free speech and gives unlimited power to the executive to censor any speech.

Article 20 talks of protection in respect of conviction for offences. It has three sub clauses.

(1) No person shall be convicted of any offence except for violation of a law in force at the time of the commission of the Act charged as an offence, nor be subjected to a penalty greater than that which might have been inflicted under the law in force at the time of the commission of the offence.

(2) No person shall be prosecuted and punished for the same offence more than once.

(3) No person accused of any offence shall be compelled to be a witness against himself.

Article 20(1) states that every penal offence made by the legislature shall only be applicable prospectively and not retrospectively. Ex post facto operation of penal laws has been declared unconstitutional by this Article. In simpler words, this Article provides that a person can be held guilty of only those offence, which had been declared to be so at the time when such offence was committed. The principle behind it is that 'no one can be held guilty of an offence which does not exist as an offence on the day when it was committed'.

Article 20(2) provides for protection against 'double jeopardy'. According to this Article, a person once convicted for an offence shall not be tried for that same offence on the basis of same facts on which he/she was previously convicted. The legal principle behind this Article is that 'no person shall be vexed twice for the same offence'. In Latin this is called 'Nemo Debet Bis Vexari'.

Article 20(3) provides every person right against self-incrimination. It is modelled on the Fifth Amendment to American Constitution which states 'no person shall be compelled in any criminal case to be a witness against himself'. According to this Article, no person who has been accused of an offence shall be compelled to depose against him/her self or be a witness against themselves in a court of law.

In the case of *M.P Sharma vs Satish Chandra (1954)* the accused were charged with offence of fraud. In pursuance of the investigation multiple places were searched and documents seized under the authority of search warrants. The accused sought relief from the court in the form of quashing of the search warrants as they claimed that the private documents seized during such searches violated their right against self-incrimination given under Article 20(3) of the Constitution. Two questions that were raised before the Supreme Court in this case are as follows:

(a) Whether compelling production of evidence, both oral and documentary, by a witness amounts to self-incrimination under Article 20 (3)?

(b) Whether search and seizure through warrants amount to violation of Article 20 (3)?

To the first question the court answered in 'yes'. It held that there exists a difference between 'being a witness' and 'furnishing evidence'. A witness is required to give information which is personal to him/her. A witness has a complete right over such knowledge or information and he/she can choose not to share it with others. Whereas furnishing evidence only amounts to producing relevant material to the case. Also, search is carried by the police officer. The evidence collected during search cannot be called incriminatory in themselves but become incriminatory only if there exists other relevant facts and circumstances. Based upon the same reasoning the court answered the second question in 'no'. The court held that search and seizure through warrants do not amount to violation of right given under Article 20 (3).

19

D K Basu vs State of West Bengal (1997) 1 SCC 416

In case of arrest and detention, guidelines are to be followed.

Facts: DK Basu addressed a letter to the Supreme Court of India calling his attention to certain news about deaths in police custody and custody. On 14/08/1987 the Court issued the Order issuing notices to all state governments and a notice was also issued to the Law Commission requesting appropriate suggestions within a two-month period.

Decision: Article 21 guarantees the right to life and personal liberty and has been held to include the right to live with human dignity. It thus also includes a guarantee against torture and assault by the State or its functionaries. The Court issued a list of 11 guidelines in addition to the Constitutional and Statutory Safeguards to be followed in all cases of arrest and detention-

- Police personnel must wear precise, visible and clear identifications.
- Prepare a memorandum of arrest witnessed by at least one witness.
- Right to have a friend or relative or other person known to arrestee be informed, as soon as possible.
- Notify detainee's time, place of detention, and place of custody.
- The person arrested must be made aware of his rights.
- Case Diary shall also disclose the name of the next friend.
- The Arrestee must also be examined at the time of his arrest and major and minor injuries, if present on his body, must be recorded at that time.

- The detainee must undergo a medical examination by a trained physician every 48 hours while in custody, upon requirement.
- Copies of all documents must be sent to the Magistrate for registration.
- Arrestee be allowed to meet with his attorney during the interrogation.
- Providing a Police Control Room.

20

Additional District Magistrate, Jabalpur vs Shivakant Shukla,

AIR 1976, SC 1207

During emergency, personal freedom can be curtailed.

Facts:

- 25th June, 1975 - The President in exercise of his powers which have been granted by Article 352(1) of Indian Constitution, declared that there was a grave emergency whereby security of India is threatened by the internal disturbances.
- 27th June, 1975 - By exercising the powers that are granted under Article 359 of the Constitution, it was declared that the right of any person including the foreigners to move any court in order to enforce their rights which have been granted to them under Article 14, 21 and 22 of the Constitution.
- 8th January, 1976 - By exercising the powers granted under Article 352 of Constitution, the President passed a notification declaring that right of any person to move to any court in order to enforce the right which have been granted to them under Article 19 of the Constitution.
- Several illegal detentions were made including the detention of some most prominent leaders such as Jayaprakash Narayan, Morarji Desai, Atal Bihari Vajpayee and L.K. Advani who were detained without any charges and trial.

Decision:

- Four judges except Justice Khanna were of the opinion that during the time of emergency if any action is taken by the government whether it is arbitrary or illegal, its actions cannot be questioned. This is because in such circumstances the government safeguards the life of the nation by using its extraordinary powers, and which are provided to them as emergency is also an extraordinary factor. Therefore, as liberty is a gift of law, it can also be forfeited by law.

- The purpose and objective of Article 359 (1) was to prevent the enforcement of any Fundamental Right mentioned in the Presidential order, should be suspended during the emergency. Even the application for Habeas Corpus under Article 491 of Code of Criminal Procedure cannot be filed simultaneously before the High Court.
- Dissenting Opinion: The state has got no power to deprive any person of their life and liberty without the authority of law, even in the absence of Article 21. It is with a view to balancing the conflicting viewpoints that the framers of the Constitution made express provisions for preventive detention and at the same time inserted safeguards to prevent abuse of those powers and to mitigate the harshness of those provisions.

21

Smt. Selvi vs State of Karnataka (2010) 7 SCC 263

Narco Analysis Test cannot be administered involuntarily.

In this case, the constitutionality of Narco Analysis Test was put to question before the court. The court held that compulsory extraction of evidence through such a test is unconstitutional and violates the right against self-incrimination given under Article 20 (3). The court held that such test when administered involuntarily in unconstitutional.

Article 21

No person shall be deprived of his life or personal liberty except according to procedure established by law.

This Article guarantees right to life and personal liberty. However, it is not absolute right. It can be restricted according to the procedure established by law. This procedure which takes away the personal liberty of a person shall be reasonable enough as contemplated under Article 19 to pass the test of being due process of law, which means a non-arbitrary, just, fair, and reasonable process. Article 21 reads: No person shall be deprived of his life or personal liberty except according to the procedure established by law. The phrase 'procedure established by law' was vividly debated by the constituent assembly. The main debate was regarding whether procedure established by law or the due process of law shall prevail when it comes to depriving citizens of their right to personal liberty. Ultimately the assembly decided upon the phrase 'procedure established by law'. Hence, legislature could take away personal liberty of the citizens by passing a legislation providing for the same. The role of judiciary was limited only to examining whether the procedure prescribed by such a legislation are duly followed.

(1) R.C. Cooper vs Union of India (1970)

(2) Kharak Singh vs State of U.P. (1963)

(3) Maneka Gandhi vs Union of India (1978)

22

A.K. Gopalan vs State of Madras

AIR 1950 SC 27

Each fundamental right is to be judged separately.

Facts: This was first time when the Supreme Court of India had to take up its role of interpreter of the Constitution and make an interpretation about the fundamental rights. In this case, a political activist was detained under the Preventive Detention Act, 1950. In his pleading before the court he had claimed that his detention under the Preventive Detention Act was in violation of his fundamental right of movement under Article 19 (1) (d) which was a constituent of right to personal liberty under Article 21. It was argued before the court that the fundamental rights shall be read collectively and not in isolation. Therefore, if a legislation that provided for taking away of personal liberty of citizen violated any other fundamental right given under part three of the Constitution then such law shall be declared unconstitutional.

Issue: Are fundamental rights to be read in isolation or in harmony with the other fundamental rights given under part three of the Constitution?

Decision: The court, doing a strict reading of the phrase 'procedure established by law' under Article 21, held that when the violation of one of the fundamental rights is challenged, its Constitutionality is not to be judged with respect to other fundamental rights. Rejecting petitioner's contention, the court was of the view that the fundamental rights shall be read in isolation and not in harmony with other fundamental rights.

However, in its later decisions, the court departed from its judgement in the Gopalan Case. In *R.C. Cooper vs Union of India (1970)* the court held that right to life and liberty given under Article 21 is to be read harmoniously with other fundamental rights given under part three of the Constitution. Hence the freedoms granted to a person under Article 19 do not cease to exist if such person is detained in accordance with the law prescribed under Article 21.

Such liberal and harmonious reading of fundamental rights continued in the case of *Kharak Singh vs State of Uttar Pradesh (1963)*.

23

Maneka Gandhi vs Union of India AIR 1978, SC 597

Due process of law will be recognized.

This case arose in the aftermath of one of the darkest phases of the Indian judiciary, the national emergency. It was the time when the confidence of the citizenry in the independence of the judiciary was shaken. The verdict pronounced by the Supreme Court in the case of ADM Jabalpur/ Habeas Corpus Case had cast a blot on the image of judiciary.

Facts: Maneka Gandhi, the daughter in law of former Prime Minister Indira Gandhi ran a magazine which published material critical of the then government and its minsters. She had to travel abroad to attend a talk but before she could board her flight, her passport was seized by the authorities in 'public interest' under section 10 (3) (c) of the Passports Act. She then requested authorities for a reasoned order behind the seizing of her passport but her request was declined.

Issue: Is phrase 'procedure established by law' to be read strictly?

Decision: The case was decided by a seven judge Constitutional bench. The bench decided that procedure by which a person is to be deprived of personal liberty has to be just, fair and reasonable. And it cannot be oppressive, fanciful and arbitrary. The court in this case also held the right to travel abroad to be fundamental right under the scope of Article 21. At the end, the court held that the government order under which Mrs. Gandhi's passport was impounded was arbitrary and violated various fundamental rights such freedom of movement under Article 19 and right to equality under Article 14. Hence, it was declared unconstitutional by the court. This was the first time in the history of Indian Judiciary that the American principle of 'due process of law' prevailed over 'the procedure established by law'.

24

Olga Tellis vs Bombay Municipal Corporation (1985)

Human right can have same protection as fundamental right.

Human Rights are the minimum basic rights that are necessary for dignified life. They can be divided into three types/generations- first generation human rights, also called civil and political rights; second generation human rights or economic, social and cultural; and third generation human rights/collective and solidarity rights. When the Constitution of India was framed it incorporated only the first generational civil and political rights in the form of fundamental rights. The second generational human rights were put in part four of the Constitution under the heading of Directive Principles of State Policy. This is the non-justiciable part of the Constitution.

In the initial decades, courts only upheld the first-generation human rights, i.e. the rights given under part three of the Constitution. However, in the later decades, with the rise of activism in Indian judiciary, the court began enforcing the second-generation human rights by reading them as an inherent part of right to life under Article 21 of the Constitution. One such case was the Olga Tellis case where the court held the right to shelter to slum dwellers as a fundamental right under Article 21.

Facts: In 1981, Bombay Municipal Corporation started an eviction drive against the pavement dwellers under Sections 312-14 of the BMC act. The drive was challenged before the Supreme Court.

Decision: Petitioners in this case argued that slum dwellers had a right to life and liberty under Article 21 of the Constitution and right to livelihood is inherent under right to life. The court accepted this argument and affirmed right to shelter to slum dwellers is a fundamental right under Article 21. The court stated that such right can be taken away only through procedure established by law. Such procedure however shall be just, fair and reasonable. The court stated that the procedure prescribed by Sections 312-14 of the BMC Act under which eviction drive was being carried was just, fair, and reasonable and hence Constitutionally valid too. Therefore the court permitted the eviction drive.

25

K.S. Puttaswamy Justice (Retd.) vs Union of India
2015 (8) SCC 735
Issuance of Aadhar Card is not violation of right to privacy.

Facts: This case is also known as the Aadhar case as the Constitutional validity of the Aadhar Act was challenged in this case. Aadhar Act provided for collection of biometrics of a person for the Aadhar card and made the card necessary for claiming several government benefits. The Act was challenged on the grounds that collection and storing of sensitive information such as biometrics of an individual amounted to violation of his/her right to privacy. The matter was heard by a nine-judge bench.

Issue: Is right to privacy a fundamental right?

Decision: In this case, the court reversed the findings of the eight-judge bench in *M.P. Sharma vs Satish Chandra (1954)* and four judge bench in *Kharak Singh vs State of U.P. (1964)* where they held that right to privacy was not a fundamental right. In Puttaswamy, the court adjudged that Right to privacy is a fundamental right under right to life and liberty as provided under Article 21 of the Constitution. This judgment went on to form the bedrock of the judgment in the case of Navtej Johar where court decriminalized homosexuality.

The Supreme Court also observed as below:

Menace of corruption and black money has reached alarming proportion in this country. It is eating into the economic progress which the country is otherwise achieving. It is not necessary to go into the various reasons for this menace. However, it would be pertinent to comment that even as per the observations of the Special Investigation Team (SIT) on black money headed by Justice M.B. Shah, one of the reasons is that persons have the option to quote their PAN or UID or passport number or driving licence or any other proof of identity while entering into financial/ business transactions. Because of this multiple methods of giving proofs of identity, there is no mechanism/system at present to collect the data available with each of the independent proofs of ID. For this reason, even SIT suggested that these databases be interconnected. To the same effect is the recommendation of the Commiottee headed by Chairman, CBDT on measures to tackle black money in India and abroad which also discusses the problem of money-laundering being done to evade taxes under the garb of shell companies by the persons who hold multple bogus PAN numbers under different names or variations of their names. That can be possible if one uniform proof of identity, namely, UID is adopted. It may go a long way to check and minimise the said malaise.

Aadhaar or UID, which has come to be known as most advanced and sophisticated infrastructure, may facilitate law enforcement agencies to take care of problem of terrorism to some extent and may also be helpful in checking the crime and also help investigating agencies in cracking the crimes. No doubt, going by aforesaid, and may be some other similarly valid considerations, it is the intention of the Government to give phillip to Aadhaar movement and encourage the people of this country to enroll themselves under the Aadhaar scheme.

26

Anita Kushwaha vs Pushap Sudan

(2016) 8 SCC 509

Access to justice is a right to life.

Facts: The transfer petitions are opposed by the respondents, *inter alia*, on the ground that the provisions of Section 25 of the Code of Civil Procedure and Section 406 of the Code of Criminal Procedure, which empower this Court to direct transfer of civil and criminal cases respectively from one State to the other, do not extend to the State of Jammu and Kashmir. Further, the Jammu and Kashmir Code of Civil Procedure, 1977 and the Jammu and Kashmir Code of Criminal Procedure, 1989 do not contain any provision empowering the Supreme Court to direct transfer of any case from that State to a Court outside the State or in the absence of any provision empowering this Court to direct transfer of civil or criminal cases from or to the State of Jammu and Kashmir, no such power can be invoked or exercised by this Court.

Decision: There is no prohibition against the use of power under Article 142 to direct transfer of cases from a Court in the State of Jammu and Kashmir to a Court outside the State or *vice versa*. The absence of an enabling provision, however, cannot be construed as a prohibition against transfer of cases to or from the State of Jammu and Kashmir. What is equally important is to see whether there is any fundamental principle of the public policy underlying any such prohibition. Neither such prohibition nor any public policy can be seen in the cases at hand much less a public policy based on any fundamental principle. The provisions of Articles 32, 136 and 142 are, therefore, wide enough to empower this Court to direct such transfer in appropriate situations, no matter Central Code of Civil and Criminal Procedures do not extend to the State nor do the State Codes of Civil and Criminal Procedure contain any provision that empowers this court to transfer cases. The Court added that, "If "life" implies not only life in the physical sense but a bundle of rights that makes life worth living, there is no juristic or other basis for holding that denial of "access to justice" will not affect the quality of human life so as to take access to justice out of the purview of right to life guaranteed under Article 21. We have, therefore, no hesitation in holding that access to justice is indeed a facet of right to life guaranteed under Article 21 of the Constitution."

27

Subhash Sharma vs Union of India

AIR 1991 SC 631

Sanctioned strength of judges should be maintained.

There is a big backlog of cases in every court, causing delays, expenses and distress to lakhs of litigants throughout the country. The Supreme Court is also burdened with arrears. At one time, there were only half the sanctioned number of judges. Appointments of judges are often caught in politics as the appointing authorities—the executive, the Chief Justices of the high courts and the Supreme Court—pull in different directions. These three petitions sought a remedy for this problem.

Facts: The petitions were filed by lawyer Subhash Sharma, the Supreme Court Advocates-on-Record Association and the honorary secretary of the Bombay Bar Association. They asked the court to direct the Union Government to fill up the vacancies in the Supreme Court and the high courts.

Ruling: The Union Government challenged the maintainability of the petition arguing that this was not a matter in which the court can pass orders. But the court overruled it and stated that once the sanctioned strength was determined, it was the obligation of the Central Government to maintain the sanctioned strenght.

The petitions were filed in 1985 and the court adjourned the hearings from time to time with interim directions calling upon the Union Government to fill up the vacancies within specified dates. As a result of this monitoring by interim directions, the position eased somewhat by 1991. But with retirements and other related developments, the number of vacancies kept increasing. This should be remedied.

The judgement goes into the detailed aspects of judges' appointments. It was not satisfied with its 1981 ruling on the position of the Chief Justice of India in the consultation process and fixation of judges' strength. Therefore, it referred those two questions to a bench of nine Supreme Court judges for reconsideration.

28

Romila Thapar vs Union of India

(2018) 10 SCC 802

Demand for special investigation is not permissible.

Facts: On 28th August, the Maharashtra Police had carried out simultaneous raids across different parts of India, resulting in the arrest of five activists: Vara Vara Rao, Sudha Bhardwaj, Gautam Navalakha, Vernon Gonzalves and Arun Farreira. The Maharashtra Police alleged that the activists were responsible for the Elgaar Parishad, which allegedly had triggered the Bhima Koregaon violence. The Police claimed that the activists are members of the Communist Party of India (Maoist), a banned organization. The Bhima Koregaon violence refers to violence during an annual celebratory gathering on 01. 01. 2018 at Bhima Koregaon to mark the 200th anniversary of the Battle of Bhima Koregaon. The violence and stone pelting by anti-social elements on the gathering resulted in death of a 28-year old youth and injury to five others. The annual celebration, also called Elgar Parishad convention, was organised by retired justices B.G Kolte-Patil and P.. B. Sawant. Justice P. B. Sawant claimed that the term "Elgar" meant loud invitation or loud declaration. On 30. 08. 2018, Romila Thapar, Devaki Jain, Prabhat Patnaik, Satish Deshpande and Maja Dharuwala submitted a joint petition to the Supreme Court challenging the arbitrary arrests of the August arresttees. The petitioners contended that the Police had violated the activists' rights to equality before the law (Article 14), free expression (Article 19) and personal liberty (Article 21). They argued that the arrests were arbitrarily made to curb dissent. They emphasised that the activists had been booked under the draconian UAPA. Further, the Maharashtra Police had made serious procedural lapses during the raids.

Decision: Majority rejected the plea for conducting the enquiry by the Special Investigation Team (SIT) regarding the arrest of five Human Rights activists. *The rejection can be referred from the case of Narmada Bai vs. State of Gujarat and Ors.* where the court stated that the parties to the case cannot determine the investigation bureau as per their own personal choice and preference. Supreme Court elongated the house arrest for the four years. The court held that authorities had produced sufficient and relevant evidences and disagreed with the contention that the arrest was made with the lack of evidence.

Babu Singh vs State of U.P.
1978 AIR 527
Speedy justice is a fundamental right.

Facts: All the petitioners were charged with the offence of murder u/s 302 I.P.C., but all of them were acquitted by the Sessions Judge on 04.11.1972. The State successfully appealed against the acquittal and by its judgment dated 20.05.1977 the High Court, while reversing the findings of the Sessions Court, held all of them guilty and sentenced them all to life imprisonment. The petitioners came up to the Supreme Court exercising their statutory right of appeal. Pending the disposal of the appeal, they moved an application for bail which was rejected on 07.09.1977. The petitioners moved another application for bail.

Judgement:

- The significance and sweep of Art. 21 make the deprivation of liberty ephemeral or enduring, a matter of grave concern and permissible only when the law authorising it is reasonable, even handed and geared to the goals of community good and State-necessity spelt out. In Article 19, reasonableness postulates intelligent care and predicates that deprivation of freedom by refusal of bail is not for punitive purpose, but for the bifocal interests of justice to the individual involved and society affected.
- Our justice, system, even in grave cases, suffers from slow motion syndrome which is lethal to "fair trial"., whatever the ultimate decision' Speedy justice is a component of social justice since the community, as a whole, is concerned in the criminal being condignly and finally punished within a reasonable and the innocent being absolved from the inordinate ordeal of criminal proceedings.

30

Hussainara Khatoon vs Home Secretary, State of Bihar

1979 AIR 1369

Undertrial prisoners cannot be kept beyond maximum period of their punishment.

Facts:

- The writ petition has come before the Court for the hearing of the release of under-trial prisoners in the state of Bihar. The state of Bihar was directed to file a revised chart showing a year-wise break-up of the under-trial prisoners after dividing into two broad categories viz. minor offenses and major offenses that were not carried out.
- It has been averred in the counter-affidavit to the direction of the Court that many under-trial prisoners, petitioners herein, confined in the Patna Central Jail, the Muzaffarpur Central Jail and the Ranchi Central Jail, prior to their release have been regularly produced before the Magistrates numerous times and have been remanded again and again to judicial custody by them.

Decision:

- The Court directed that these under-trial prisoners whose names and particulars are given in the list filed should be released forthwith as continuance of their detention is illegal and in violation of their fundamental right under Article 21 of the Constitution because they have been in jail for a duration exceeding the maximum term that they should have been convicted for.
- The Court found that the under-trial prisoners whose list was filed before the Court have been in jail for periods

longer than the maximum term for which they could have been sentenced if convicted. The Court recognized the callousness of the legal and judicial system and unjustified deprivation of personal liberty. The Court also realized the plight of under-trial prisoners who are for most times, unaware of their right to obtain release on bail or due to poverty, are unable to engage a lawyer. For this, the need for an adequate and comprehensive legal service program is called for.

- The emphasis is laid towards the under-trial prisoners who have been in jail for more than half the maximum term of imprisonment for which they could be sentenced if convicted. There is no reason why these under-trial prisoners should be allowed to continue to languish in jail, merely because of the fault of the State to not try them within a reasonable period of time. The possibility of some of them being acquitted of the offenses charged against them yet having spent several years in jail for offenses which they are ultimately found not to have committed will be detrimental to their freedom of personal liberty. Hence, the speedy trial of persons accused of offenses becomes essential to ensure that the accused persons do not have to remain in jail longer than is absolutely necessary.

31

State of Punjab and Others vs Jagjit Singh and Others

AIR 2016 SC 5176 = 2017 (1) SCC 148

Equal Pay for Equal work

Facts: All the judgments noticed in paragraphs 7 to 24 hereinabove, pertain to employees engaged on regular basis, who were claiming higher wages, under the principle of 'equal pay for equal work'. The claim raised by such employees was premised on the ground, that the duties and responsibilities rendered by them, were against the same post for which a higher pay-scale was being allowed, in other Government departments. Or alternatively, their duties and responsibilities were the same, as of other posts with different designations, but they were placed in a lower scale. Having been painstakingly taken through the parameters laid down by this Court, wherein the principle of 'equal pay for equal work' was invoked and considered, it would be just and appropriate, to delineate the parameters laid down by this Court. In recording the said parameters, we have also adverted to some other judgments pertaining to temporary employees (also dealt with, in the instant judgment), wherein also, this Court had the occasion to express the legal position with reference to the principle of 'equal pay for equal work'.

Ruling: Given the fact that pronouncements mentioned above have interpreted and understood the word "life" appearing in Article 21 of the Constitution on a broad spectrum of rights considered incidental and/or integral to the right to life, there is no real reason why access to justice should be considered to be falling outside the class and category of the said rights, which already stands recognised as being a part and parcel of the Article 21 of the Constitution of India.

If "life" implies not only life in the physical sense but a bundle of rights that makes life worth living, there is no juristic or other basis for holding that denial of "access to justice" will not affect the quality of human life so as to take access to justice out of the purview of right to life guaranteed under Article 21. We have, therefore, no hesitation in holding that access to justice is indeed a facet of right to life guaranteed under Article 21 of the Constitution. We need only add that access to justice may as well be the facet of the right guaranteed under Article 14 of the Constitution, which guarantees equality before law and equal protection of laws to not only citizens but non-citizens also. We say so because equality before law and equal protection of laws is not limited in its application to the realm of executive action that enforces the law. It is as much available in relation to proceedings before Courts and tribunal and adjudicatory for a where law is applied and justice administered. The Citizen's inability to access courts or any other adjudicatory mechanism provided for determination of rights and obligations is bound to result in denial of the guarantee contained in Article 14 both in relation to equality before law as well as equal protection of laws. Absence of any adjudicatory mechanism or the inadequacy of such mechanism, needless to say, is bound to prevent those looking for enforcement of their right to equality before laws and equal protection of the laws from seeking redress and thereby negate the guarantee of equality before laws or equal protection of laws and reduce it to a mere teasing illusion. Article 21 of the Constitution apart, access to justice can be said to be part of the guarantee contained in Article 14 as well.

Four main facets that, constitute the essence of access to justice are:

(i) The State must provide an effective adjudicatory mechanism;

(ii) The mechanism so provided must be reasonably accessible in terms of distance;

(iii) The process of adjudication must be speedy; and

(iv) The litigant's access to the adjudicatory process must be affordable.

(i) The need for adjudicatory mechanism

One of the most fundamental requirements for providing to the citizens access to justice is to set-up an adjudicatory mechanism whether described as a Court, Tribunal, Commission or Authority or called by any other name whatsoever, where a citizen can agitate his grievance and seek adjudication of what he may perceive as a breach of his right by another citizen or by the State or any one of its instrumentalities. In order that the right of a citizen to access justice is protected, the mechanism so provided must not only be effective but must also be just, fair and objective in its approach. So also the procedure which the court, Tribunal or Authority may adopt for adjudication, must, in itself be just and fair and in keeping with the well recognized principles of natural justice.

(ii) The mechanism must be conveniently accessible in terms of distance:

The forum/mechanism so provided must, having regard to the hierarchy of courts/tribunals, be reasonably accessible in terms of distance for access to justice since so much depends upon the ability of the litigant to place his/her grievance effectively before the court/tribunal/court/competent authority to grant such a relief.!

(iii) The process of adjudication must be speedy.

"Access to justice" as a constitutional value will be a mere illusion if justice is not speedy. Justice delayed, it is famously said, is justice denied. If the process of administration of justice is so time consuming, laborious, indolent and frustrating for those who seek justice that it dissuades or deters them from even considering resort to that process as an option, it would tantamount to denial of not only access to justice but justice itself. In Sheela Barse's case (supra) this Court declared speedy trial as a facet of right to life, for if the trial of a citizen goes on endlessly his right to life itself is violated. There is jurisprudentially no qualitative difference between denial of speedy trial in a criminal case, on the one hand, and civil suit, appeal or other proceedings, on the other hand, we know that civil disputes can at times have an equally, if not, more severe impact on a citizen's life or the quality of it. Access to Justice would, therefore, be a constitutional value of any significance and utility only if the delivery of justice to the citizen is speedy, for otherwise, the right to access to justice is no more than a hollow slogan of no use or inspiration for the citizen. It is heartening to note that over the past six decades or so the number of courts established in the country has increased manifold in comparison to the number that existed on the day the country earned its freedom. There is today almost invariably a court of Civil Judge junior or senior division in every taluka and a District and Sessions Judge in every district. In terms of accessibility from the point of view of distance which a citizen ought to travel, we have come a long way since the time the British left the country, However, the increase in literacy, awareness, prosperity and proliferation of laws has made the process of adjudication slow and time consuming primarily on account of the over worked and under staffed judicial system, which is crying for creation of additional courts with requisite human resources and infrastructure to effectively deal with an ever increasing number of cases being filed in the courts and mounting backlog of over thirty million cases in the subordinate courts. While the States have done their bit in terms of providing the basic adjudicatory mechanisms for disposal of resolution of civil or criminal conflicts, access to justice remains a big question mark on account of delays in the completion of the process of adjudication on account of poor judge population and judge case ratio in comparison to other countries.

(iv) The process of adjudication must be affordable to the disputants:

Access to justice will again be no more than an illusion if the adjudicatory mechanism provided is so expensive as to deter a disputant from taking resort to the same. Article 39-A of the Constitution promotes a laudable objective of providing legal aid to needy litigants and obliges the State to make access to justice affordable for the less fortunate sections of the society. Legal aid to the needy has been recognized as one of the facets of access to justice in Madhav Hayawadanrao Hoskot vs State of Maharashtra, where this court observed:

"If a prisoner sentenced to imprisonment, is virtually unable to exercise his constitutional and statutory right of appeal, inclusive of special leave to appeal, for want of legal assistance, there is implicit in the Court under Art. 142, read with Arts. 21, and 39A of the Constitution, power to assign counsel for such imprisoned individual for doing complete justice. This is a necessary incident of the right of appeal conferred by the Code and allowed by Art. 136 of the Constitution. The inference is inevitable that this is a State's duty and not government's charity. Equally affirmative is the implication that while legal services must be free to the beneficiary, the lawyer himself has to be reasonably remunerated for his services. Surely, the profession has a public commitment to the people but mere philanthropy of its members yields short mileage in the long run. Their services, especially when they are on behalf of the State, must be paid for. Naturally, the State concerned must pay a reasonable sum that the court may fix when assigning counsel to the prisoner. Of course, the court may judge the situation and consider from all angles whether it is necessary for the ends of justice to make availale legal aid in the particular case.

32

Gian Kaur vs State of Punjab 1996 SSC (2) 648

Right to life does not include right to die.

In this case the court overruled the judgment in the P. Rathinam vs Union of India and declared Section 309 of IPC to be Constitutional. Right to life does not include right to die and attempt to commit suicide was again made a culpable offence.

The Golden Triangle of Articles 14, 19 and 21

Before the judgments in the cases of R.C. Cooper and Maneka Gandhi the court in the A.K. Gopalan case had held that fundamental rights shall not be read in conjunction with each other but in isolation. However, later this practice was overturned and court began reading the fundamental rights in the light of the entire part three of the Constitution. Hence emerged the **Golden Triangle of Articles 14, 19 and 21**. Every law whose Constitutionality is to be ascertained on the grounds of any of these three Articles has to pass the test of Constitutionality prescribed by the rest two Articles too. For e.g. if a law is to be tested whether it violates Article 21 or not, such law shall also be adjudged on the altar of Articles 14 and 19 too.

Article 22 is titled 'protection against arrest and detention'. As the name suggests, this Article provides for several procedural requirements which ensure protection against unlawful arrests and detentions.

(1) No person who is arrested shall be detained in custody without being informed, as soon as may be, of the grounds for such arrest nor shall he be denied the right to consult, and to be defended by, a legal practitioner of his choice.

(2) Every person who is arrested and detained in custody shall be produced before the nearest magistrate within a period

of twenty-four hours of such arrest excluding the time necessary for the journey from the place of arrest to the court of the magistrate and no such person shall be detained in custody beyond the said period without the authority of a magistrate.

(3) Nothing in clauses (1) and (2) shall apply— (a) to any person who for the time being is an enemy alien; or (b) to any person who is arrested or detained under any law providing for preventive detention.

**(4) No law providing for preventive detention shall authorise the detention of a person for a longer period than three months unless— (a) an Advisory Board consisting of persons who are, or have been, or are qualified to be appointed as, Judges of a High Court has reported before the expiration of the said period of three months that there is in its opinion sufficient cause for such detention:

Provided that nothing in this sub-clause shall authorise the detention of any person beyond the maximum period prescribed by any law made by Parliament under sub-clause (b) of clause (7); or (b) such person is detained in accordance with the provisions of any law made by Parliament under sub clauses (a) and (b) of clause (7).

(5) When any person is detained in pursuance of an order made under any law providing for preventive detention, the authority making the order shall, as soon as may be, communicate to such person the grounds on which the order has been made and shall afford him the earliest opportunity of making a representation against the order.

(6) Nothing in clause (5) shall require the authority making any such order as is referred to in that clause to disclose facts which such authority considers to be against the public interest to disclose.

(7) Parliament may by law prescribe— * (a) the circumstances under which, and the class or classes of cases in which,

a person may be detained for a period longer than three months under any law providing for preventive detention without obtaining the opinion of an Advisory Board in accordance with the provisions of sub-clause (a) of clause (4); ** (b) the maximum period for which any person may in any class or classes of cases be detained under any law providing for preventive detention; and (c) the procedure to be followed by an Advisory Board in an inquiry under ***[sub-clause (a) of clause(4)].

It mentions different procedures that every law which aims to curtail an individual's right of life and liberty through arrest or detention shall follow.

The mandate of Article 22 is to control detention under two kinds of law. While clauses 1 and 2 of this Article deal with rights of the person arrested under an ordinary criminal law, clauses 3 to 7 deal with rights of the person arrested under a preventive detention law.

Article 23 is titled 'prohibition of traffic in human beings and forced labour'. This Article prohibits traffic in human beings; beggar; and any other forms of labour.

Article 24 is titled 'prohibition of employment of children in factories, etc.'

Right to Freedom of Religion (Articles 25-28)

Religion is an important aspect of lives in India. It forms part of every aspect of both personal and political lives in the country. When Constitution was being drafted rights relating to freedom of religion, both for the society and the person were put under the heading 'Right to Freedom of Religion' from Articles 25 to 28. It was through the 42ndAmendment Act that the word 'secular' was added to the preamble of the Constitution. In the S.R. Bommai case (1994), the Supreme Court held that the word 'secularism' was a part of the basic feature of the Constitution.

Article 25 is titled **'freedom of conscience and free profession, practice and propagation of religion'**.

(1) Subject to public order, morality and health and to the other provisions of this Part, all persons are equally entitled to freedom of conscience and the right freely to profess, practise and propagate religion.

(2) Nothing in this Article shall affect the operation of any existing law or prevent the State from making any law—(a) regulating or restricting any economic, financial, political or other secular activity which may be associated with religious practice; (b) providing for social welfare and reform or the throwing open of Hindu religious institutions of a public character to all classes and sections of Hindus.

Explanation I.—The wearing and carrying of kirpans shall be deemed to be included in the profession of the Sikh religion.

Explanation II. —In sub-clause (b) of clause (2), the reference to Hindus shall be construed as including a reference to persons professing the Sikh, Jain or Buddhist religion, and the reference to Hindu religious institutions shall be construed accordingly.

Article 25(1) allows people not only to follow a religion of their choice but also to act in pursuance of their religion in the manner they deem fit. But the exercise of these rights is subject to some reasonable restrictions such as public order, health and morality. Following are the three broad rights available under this Article- Freedom of conscience, freedom to profess, and freedom to practice religion.

Clause two of Article 25, *i.e.* Article 25(2) allows state to regulate secular activities associated with religion. However, the word 'secular' is not defined anywhere in the Constitution. Article 25(2) (a) gives state the power to regulate secular activities, such as economic, financial, political etc. associated with the religion.

Article 25(2) (b) gives to the state power of throwing open any Hindu temple/ institution for all castes of Hindus. This clause gives state the power to carry out social reform.

Article 26 is titled 'freedom to manage religious affairs'. It provides all religious denominations and religious sects the power to manage its own religious affairs; to buy and administer in accordance with law property, both moveable and immoveable. Exercise of freedom under this Article is also subject to the reasonable restrictions of public order, health and morality.

Article 27 is titled as 'freedom from payment of taxes for promotion of any particular religion'.

Article 28 is titled 'freedom as to attendance at religious instructions or religious worship in certain educational institutions'.

Essential Religious Practice Test

As can be seen from a bare reading of the texts of Articles 25 and 26 that while Article 25 deals with right to freedom of practice and propagation of religion of an individual, Article 26 on the other hand provides for freedom to manage the religious affairs by a sect or denomination. But what when the two rights, i.e. of an individual and of the community clash with each other. The provisions for the same cannot be found in the Constitution. Soon after independence, the court began facing such cases where right to freedom of religion of an individual and right to manage its religious affairs by a sect were at loggerheads with each other. To decide such cases, the court came up with the Essential Religious Practice Test. According to this test, court provided Constitutional protection to only those practices which it deemed to be essential to the religion. This test underwent several changes over a number of cases. However, till date, this test remains one of the most debated tests prescribed by the court. Different benches of court have interpreted it differently with no clear consensus over it. The mention of the term 'essentially religious' is also found in the words of B.R. Ambedkar in the constituent assembly debates where he proclaimed the meaning of the term religion as used in the Part three of the Constitution shall not extend beyond belief and rituals that are considered to be 'essential to the religion'.

33

Sardar Syedna Taher Saifuddin Saheb vs State of Bombay (1962) AIR 853

State can not interfere in excommunication matter.

Facts: In this case, the Bombay Prevention of Excommunication Act, 1949 was challenged before the Supreme Court. This Excommunication Act declared illegal, any kind of excommunication within any religious community. Excommunication is the practice of barring a person from access to the membership of the religious community to which he/she earlier belonged. It is often done by a body or by the head of a sect. The head of the sect of Dawoodi Bohra community which is an offshoot of the Shia Islam challenged this Prevention of Excommunication Act in the Supreme Court. His main contention was that this Act took away his power of excommunicating someone from the sect. This was a violation of sect's right to manage its religious affairs given under Article 26 (b) of the Constitution.

Decision: The court accepted the contentions of the petitioners with a 4-1 majority and struck down the impugned Act. It was held that Articles 25 and 26 gave protection to the essential practices of a religion and on the basis of the authorities cited. It was held that sect's power to excommunicate was an essential religious practice.

Hence, after this case evolved a two-step test to verify whether a practice passes the essential religious practice test or not. The first step was to see whether the practice in question was religious or secular in nature? If it was a religious practice then the next step was to see whether the practice was essential to the religion or not?

However, the scope of this test was widened to include the word integral to it. In the case of *Dargah Committee, Ajmer vs Syed Hussain Ali (1962),* it was held that for a practice to be treated as a Constitutionally protected part of the religion then such practice shall be both 'essential and integral' to the religion. Basically, in this case the two-step test as prescribed in earlier cases was scrapped and the two steps were merged in one test, i.e. 'essential and integral test'. Hence the scope for judicial intervention was substantially increased.

What is a religious denomination?

The meaning if the term 'religious denomination' used in Article 26 was explained in the case of *S.P. Mittal vs Union of India (1983)*. In this case, the petitioners, followers of Sri Aurobindo Society, had challenged the Constitutionality of the Aurobindo Act. The act provided for the taking over of a township named Auroville which was being developed by the Aurobindo Society. The petitioners contended that the impugned act violated their right to freedom of religion as provided to them under Article 26. It was held that to form a religious denomination for the purpose of Article 26, the following three conditions shall be fulfilled:

(1) It should be group of followers in a particular system of belief which they shall regard as integral to their spiritual wellbeing.
(2) Such group of individuals shall have a common organization.
(3) Such organization shall have a distinct name.

If a group satisfies all the three above conditions then it shall be termed 'religious denomination'. Based on this test, the court with a 4-1 majority held that Aurobindo society was not a religious denomination for the purpose of Article 26.

Cultural Educational Right

Articles 29 and 30 fall under the head 'cultural and educational rights'. It talks of guaranteeing to the minority, certain set of rights to preserve and propagate their culture. The framers of the Constitution through these rights aimed to give recognition to the diversity in the country. These values are enshrined in the word 'secular' used in the preamble.

Article 29

(1) Any section of the citizens residing in the territory of India or any part thereof having a distinct language, script or culture of its own shall have the right to conserve the same.

(2) No citizen shall be denied admission into any educational institution maintained by the State or receiving aid out of State funds on grounds only of religion, race, caste, language or any of them.

It is titled as protection of interest of minorities. Article 29(1) guarantees to people of different sect to conserve their distinct language, script and culture. The right can be exercised through different means such as establishing educational institutions, and promoting language by imparting education in such language. Article 29 (2) gives citizens right to admission into an educational education. It provides that no one shall be denied admission to an educational institution merely on the grounds of religion, race, caste, language.

Article 30 is titled 'right of minorities to establish and administer educational institutions'. This Article gives protection to both religious and linguistic minorities. Educational institutions can seek aid from the state under Article 30.

Although Articles 29 and 30 accord educational and cultural rights to minorities but Constitution does not define the word 'minority' in any of its Articles. The attempt to concretely define the term 'minority' has been made several times before the Constitution came into force. Several pre-constitutional reports such as Nehru Report (1928) and Sapru report (1945) made recommendations regarding making special provisions for minorities in the country. It was aneleven-judge bench in the case of *T.M.A. Pai Foundation vs State of Karnataka (2003)* which defined minority to be smaller of the two entity. It is a relative term and can be used in multiple senses, such as political minority, linguistic minority etc. However, in the T.M.A. Pai case the court also held that minority shall be calculated state wise and not nation wise.

34

Bachan Singh vs State of Punjab (1980) 2SCC 684

Death penalty should be given only in the rarest of the rare offences.

Facts: This Case is a landmark judgment given by 5 judges Bench of the Hon'ble Supreme Court. In this case Supreme Court announced important limitations on the death penalty by setting the "rarest of the rare" doctrine.

In this case one Bachan Singh was convicted for his wife's murder and was sentenced for life imprisonment. On his release he started living with his cousin Hukam Singh and his family. Sometime later he was tried for another offence, i.e. for the murder of his brother's wife and was sentenced to death under Section 302, Indian Penal Code by the Sessions judge. The High Court confirmed his death sentence given by the sessions judge and dismissed his appeal. Bachan Singh then appealed to the Supreme Court. The Question raised in the appeal was, whether the facts of his case qualified to be called "special reasons" as required in section 354(3) of Code of Criminal Procedure for awarding the death sentence.

The Code of Criminal Procedure specifically mentions that death sentence is to be only awarded in cases that are exceptions. It also contains a rider that if a sentence of death is awarded, the court should record special reasons for awarding the same.

Decision: The Supreme Court dismissed Bachan Singh's appeal pertaining to the constitutionality of Sec 302 of IPC and 354(3) of CRPC. The court observed that the the expression "Special reason" in section 354(3) of CRPC means "rarest of the rare cases" in awarding the death penalty. Those convicted for murder, life imprisonment is the rule and death sentence is an exception.

35

Dr. M. Ismail Faruqui vs Union of India and Others

1994 (6) SCC 360

Mosque is not an essential part of Islam.

Facts: Dr Ismail Faruqui had filed a petition challenging the validity of the Acquisition of Certain Area at Ayodhya Act, 1993, by which the Centre acquired 67.703 acres of land in and around the Babri Masjid.

Decision: The Apex Court got the petitions filed before High Court transferred, heard all the matters collectively along with the reference made under Article 143 (1) of the Constitution.

Supreme Court bench had held that a mosque was not an "essential part of the practice of the religion of Islam" and that namaz could be offered anywhere and hence, "its acquisition (by the state) is not prohibited by the provisions in the Constitution of India". The Acquisition of Certain Area at Ayodhya Act, 1993, was struck down as being unconstitutional. The writ petitions impugning the validity of the Act were allowed.

In view of the above judgment by SC, High Court proceeded to consider the Suits on merits, but with one distinction, i.e., it had reduced the area of dispute now to be considered in all these suits. The disputed area now is confined to the area within which the structure (including the premises of the inner and outer courtyards of such structure) existed. The land beyond the above is out of the scope of these suits having been validly acquired under Section 3 of the Ayodhya Act.

D.C. Wadhwa vs State of Bihar (1987) SCC (1) 378

Governor cannot issue unlimited number of ordinances.

The Governor of Bihar, between 1967 and 1981 promulgated 256 Ordinances using the ordinance making power given to the Governor under Article 213 of the Constitution. This Article permits a Governor to promulgate an ordinance during the recess of the legislature. Such ordinances must be ratified by the legislature but in this case the governor kept promulgating the same Ordinances for period ranging between one to fourteen years by re- promulgation from time to time, without getting them ratified by the house. After the session of the State legislature was prorogued, the same ordinance which had ceased to operate were re- promulgated containing substantially the same provision almost in a routine manner.

The petitioner in this case raised the question relating to the power of the Governor under Article 213 of the Constitution.

The main issue raised in this case is that does the Governor have the power to re-promulgate Ordinances time and again and in this way can the governor take over to himself the power to legislate and what are the limits of the ordinance making power of the Governor as conferred upon him under Article 213.

Judgement in the Case

The Supreme Court in this case held that the power of a Governor to promulgate an ordinance under Article 213 of the Constitution is only for the purpose of enabling him to take immediate action at a time when the legislature of the State is not in session. It is essentially a power to be used to meet an extraordinary situation and it shall not be allowed to be “perverted to serve Political ends”. The court in this case observed “The object of Article

213 is that since the power conferred on the Governor to issue Ordinances is an emergent power exercisable when the Legislature is not in session, an ordinance promulgated by the governor to deal with a situation which requires immediate action and which cannot wait until the Legislature reassembles, must necessarily have a limited life. That is why it is provided that the Ordinance shall cease to operate on the expiration of six weeks from the date of assembling of the legislature."

The judgement in this case explicitly stated that a constitutional authority cannot do indirectly what it is not permitted to do directly. Allowing the same would be a clear fraud on constitutional provision.

The Court accordingly struck down the Bihar Intermediate Education Council Ordinance, 1985, which was in operation as unconstitutional and void.

37

Navtej Singh Johar vs Union of India AIR 2018 SC 4321

Homosexuality is permissible under Section 377 of IPC.

Facts: Section 377 of Indian Penal Code penalizes the act of Homosexuality. It penalizes both consensual and nonconsensual homosexual relations. Worldwide progressive legislations have been made that allow homosexual relations. The voices demanding striking down of this oppressive colonial law grew stronger in the country. It was in this case that the Supreme Court of India struck down that part of Section 377 of Indian Penal Code which penalized the consensual Homosexual relations. The matter reached Supreme Court through a writ petition. A five-judge bench of the Supreme Court presided over the matter. The petition demanded for declaration of "right to sexuality", "right to sexual autonomy" and "right to choice of a sexual partner" to be declared a part of right to life guaranteed under Article 21 of the Constitution of India. The petition also sought the Supreme Court to declare Section 377 of the Indian Penal Code as unconstitutional.

Decision: The court in this case went on to hold that Section 377 of Indian Penal Code violated the rights given under Article 14, i.e., Right To Equality as it distinguished between homosexual and heterosexual forms of sex, classifying all consensual sexual activities between non-heterosexual persons as unnatural, based simply upon their sexual orientation. The court further went on to hold that Section 377 violated freedom of expression provided under Article.19(1)(a). the reason cited for this observation was that Section 377 took away LGBT persons' freedom to express their sexuality and their choice of sexual partners. Since this judgement was pronounced after the Puttaswamy judgement where the Supreme Court declared right to privacy a fundamental right under Article 21, in this case the Supreme Court cited the Puttaswamy judgement to declare that Section 377 IPC violated the fundamental right to privacy implicit in Article 21. The Court in this case upheld the principles laid down in the Puttaswamy vs Union of India case. It recognized that Privacy includes the right to choose one's own sexual partner.

This judgement was widely celebrated around as it granted one of the most basic rights, i.e., the right to choose one's own sexual partner to homosexual adults in the country.

38

National Legal Services Authority vs Union of India

AIR 2014 SC 1863

Third gender is recognized in India.

Facts: This case was filed by the National Legal Services Authority of India (NALSA) to legally recognize persons who fall outside the male/female gender binary, including persons who identify as "third gender".

Decision: The Court has directed Centre and State Governments to grant legal recognition of gender identity whether it be male, female or third gender:

- Legal Recognition for Third Gender: The Court recognized that fundamental rights are available to the third gender in the same manner as they are to males and females. Further, non-recognition of third gender in both criminal and civil statutes such as those relating to marriage, adoption, divorce, etc. is discriminatory to the transgender.
- Legal Recognition for Persons transitioning within male/female binary: for the procedure of recognition, refer the psyche of the person and use the "Psychological Test' as opposed to the 'Biological Test'; insisting on Sex Reassignment Surgery (SRS) as a condition for changing one's gender is illegal.
- Public Health and Sanitation: medical care to transgenders in hospitals and provide them separate public toilets and other facilities. Further, separate HIV/Sero-surveillance measures for transgenders.

- Socio-Economic Rights: social welfare schemes and to treat the community as socially and economically backward classes and extend reservation in educational institutions and for public appointments.
- Stigma and Public Awareness: Centre and State Governments to take steps to create public awareness to better help incorporate transgenders into society and end treatment as untouchables; take measures to regain their respect and place in society; and seriously address the problems such as fear, shame, gender dysphoria, social pressure, depression, suicidal tendencies and social stigma.

39

Joseph Shine vs Union of India 2018 SC 1676

Section 497 of the IPC regarding adultery is unconstitutional.

Facts: In October 2017, Joseph Shine, a non-resident Keralite, filed public interest litigation under Article 32 of the Constitution. The petition challenged the constitutionality of the offence of adultery under Section 497 of the IPC read with Section 198(2) of the CrPC.

Decision: Supreme Court pronounced its judgment on constitutional validity of penal provision of adultery and ruled that "Adultery can be treated as civil wrong for dissolution of marriage, but not criminal offence". While pronouncing its judgment, the apex court said "Equality is the governing principle of a system. Husband is not the master of the wife". The court further said that "There can't be any social license which destroys a home. Adultery might not be cause of unhappy marriage, it could be result of an unhappy marriage".

- Section 497 is held to be unconstitutional as adultery is manifestly arbitrary. A law which deprives women of the right to prosecute, is not gender-neutral. Under Section 497, the wife of the adulterous male, cannot prosecute her husband for marital infidelity. This provision is, therefore, ex facie discriminatory against women, and violative of Article 14.
- The freedom to have a consensual sexual relationship outside marriage by a married person, does not warrant protection under Article 21. In the context of Article 21, an invasion of privacy by the State must be justified on the basis of a law that is reasonable and valid. Such an invasion must meet a three-fold requirement as held in Justice K. S. Puttaswamy (Retd.) & Anr. vs. UOI & Anr:
  - ❖ legality, which postulates the existence of law;
  - ❖ need, defined in terms of a legitimate State interest, and
  - ❖ proportionality, a rational nexus between the object and the means adopted.

40

P. Rathinam vs State of Gujarat & Others

1993 (2) Scale

Rape victim in police custody was awarded compensation.

Facts: In one of those cases of police atrocities, Guntaben, a tribal woman, was raped in police custody allegedly in the presence of her husband. A social worker brought the case to the attention of the Supreme Court through a regular criminal writ petition. The court appointed a commission to find out the facts. It reported that the incident was true. It pointed out the officers who had been guilty of inaction or dereliction of duty. The court was told in 1986 by the Gujarat Government that action was being taken against the guilty officers. But the government took several years to take small steps and therefore the court gave a time frame within which all enquiries must be completed and criminal proceedings should be taken.

Ruling: While the first part of the order dealt with the action to be taken against the police officers, the second part said: "A sum of ₹50,000 shall be paid as interim compensation by the State of Gujarat to the victim of the rape Smt. Guntaben, wife of Hanna Ramji. The said amount shall be deposited in the State Bank of India at Rajpipla, District Bharuch, within a period of six weeks from today.... The lady shall be free to utilise the said amount in such manner as she thinks fit."

The case was however not disposed of. The court has kept it in the live register to monitor the steps taken by the government. This is a rare case in which the Supreme Court followed up a complaint of rape for nearly a decade.

41

Tukaram vs State of Maharashtra/ Mathura Rape Case AIR 1979 SC 185

Passive resistance is not rape.

This case is popularly known as the Mathura Rape Case. It is known for setting the debate on laws relating to the offence of Rape. The judgement pronounced by the court in this case inspired huge backlash across the country. The government brought major changes to the legal definition of rape.

Facts: In 1972, the victim's brother lodged report at Desai Gunj police station claiming that his sister Mathura, had been abducted by her husband. Head Constable Baburao brought all the three persons including Mathura and her husband to the police station. In the night he asked the other two persons to leave the station whereas Mathura was asked to stay back. He then took her to a toilet and raped her. Then the other officer, Tukaram, molested and tried to rape her, but since he was too deeply drunk, he did not succeed.

The lower court held that since there were no signs of resistance on Mathura's body hence she was not raped and the sex was consensual. The Bombay High Court on appeal reversed the lower court's judgement and held that there lies a huge difference between passive submission and consent. It held, "Mere passive or helpless surrender of the body and its resignation to the other's lust induced by threats or fear cannot be equated with desire or will, nor furnish an answer by the mere fact that the sexual act was not in opposition to such desire or violation. On the other hand, taking advantage of her situation, it is more probable that the initiative for satisfying the sexual desire must've proceeded from the accused, and that mustn't have not been a willing party to the act of sexual intercourse. Her subsequent conduct in making a statement immediately not only to her relatives, but also to the members of the crowd, leave no doubt that she was subjected to forcible sexual intercourse."

The convicts went in appeal to the Supreme Court.

Decision: The Supreme Court reversed the High Court's finding and held that since no injuries were shown in the medical report hence the woman was not subjected to rape.

This judgement of the Supreme Court was heavily criticized. However, this judgment has been suitably modified subsequently in various cases.

42

Mukesh and another vs State for NCT of Delhi & Others (Nirbhaya Case) 2012 (16) SCC1

The accused of the helpless rape victims should be awarded death penalty.

Fact: The most famous case on rape with murder is of one Nirbhaya was gruesomely raped, attacked by four accused persons who were employees of a bus. While Nirbhaya, a pharmacist was travelling with her friend in that bus during the night to her home. The victim and her friend were thrown out of the bus in semi-naked condition. The victim was seriously injured and was in a critical condition. Inspite of best treatment, she succumbed to her injuries on her private parts. There was so much public cemmotion on this incident that the Courts were also influenced and this case became a landmark judgment on the such types of crimes. Ultimately, three accused were hanged and one accused person committed suicide in jail. Government of India allocated thousand of crore budget as recurring budget to all states so that such incidents are not repeated in India.

Ruling: The Supreme Court in this case judgment established that the during declaration recorded even on the basis of nods and gestures is not only admissible but possesses evidentiary value. The Supreme Court also held that discretion of Governor or President to grant clemency is also subject to judicial review and ordered for hanging of the accused which gave some satisfaction to the sentiment of general public.

Dealing with sentencing, courts have applied the "Crime Test", "Criminal Test" and the "Rarest of the Rare Test". The tests examine whether the society abhors such crimes and whether such crimes shock the conscience of the society and attract intense and extreme indignation of the community. Courts have further held that where the victims are helpless women, children or old persons and the accused displayed depraved mentality, committing crime in a diabolic manner, the accused should be shown no remorse and death penalty should be awarded.

The Supreme Court in general laid down circumstances in which rape cum murder heinous cases shuld be dealt with by courts.

Aggravating circumstances

(1) The offences relating to the commission of heinous crimes like murder, rape, armed dacoity, kidnapping, etc. by the accused with a prior record of conviction for capital felony or offences committed by the person having a substantial history of serious assaults and criminal convictions.

(2) The offence was committed while the offender was engaged in the commission of another serious offence.

(3) The offence was committed with the intention to create a fear psychosis in the public at large and was committed in a public place by a weapon or device which clearly could be hazardous to the life of more than one person.

(4) The offence of murder was committed for ransom or like offences to receive money or monetary benefits.

(5) Hired killings.

(6) The offence was committed outrageously for want only while involving inhumane treatment and torture to the victim.

(7) The offence was committed by a person while in lawful custody.

(8) The murder or the offence was committed to prevent a person lawfully carrying out his duty like arrest or custody in a place of lawful confinement of himself or another. For instance, murder is of a person who had acted in lawful discharge of his duty Under Section 43 Code of Criminal Procedure. When the crime is enormous in proportion like making an attempt of murder of the entire family or members of a particular community. When the victim is innocent, helpless or a person relies upon the trust of relationship and social norms, like a child, helpless woman, a daughter or a niece staying with a father/uncle and is inflicted with the crime by such a trusted person.

(9) When murder is committed for a motive which evidences total depravity and meanness.

(10) When there is a cold blooded murder without provocation.

(11) The crime is committed so brutally that it pricks or shocks not only the judicial conscience but even the conscience of the society.

Mitigating circumstances

(1) The manner and circumstances in and under which the offence was committed, for example, extreme mental or emotional disturbance or extreme provocation in contradistinction to all these situations in normal course.

(2) The age of the accused is a relevant consideration but not a determinative factor by itself.

(3) The chances of the accused of not indulging in commission of the crime again and the probability of the accused being reformed and rehabilitated.

(4) The condition of the accused shows that he was mentally defective and the defect impaired his capacity to appreciate the circumstances of his criminal conduct.

(5) The circumstances which, in normal course of life, would render such a behaviour possible and could have the effect of giving rise to mental imbalance in that given situation like persistent harassment or, in fact, leading to such a peak of human behaviour that, in the facts and circumstances of the case, the accused believed that he was morally justified in committing the offence.

(6) Where the court upon proper appreciation of evidence is of the view that the crime was not committed in a preordained manner and that the death resulted in the course of commission of another crime and that there was a possibility of it being construed as consequences to the commission of the primary crime.

(7) Where it is absolutely unsafe to rely upon the testimony of a sole eyewitness though the prosecution has brought home the guilt of the accused."

43

Sasanka Sekher Maity vs Union of India (1980) 4 SCC716

Conferring rights on sharecroppers or Bataidars is a public purpose.

Facts: West Bengal Government during left Rule issued guidelines for recording of sharecroppers or bargadars on lands. Some of these guidelines were also contained in the erstwhile Land Reforms Act, 1955. Following the executive order of W.B. Government about 14 lakh bargadars were recorded on the lands owned by the landowners. The landowners came to the court for protection of their land.

Decision: The Supreme Court held that a law which aims at elevating the status of tenants (sharecroppers called bargadars in West Bengal) by conferring on them 'bhoomidhan rights' (full ownership right) can not be said to be wanting in public purpose. However executive orders, are not sufficient to deprive of a person of his/her property. Similarly, the land ceiling laws/Act which ultimately confer bhoomidhan rights on landless persons after the distribution of surplus vested land beyond ceiling limit are still protected by Articles 31B and 31C of the Constitution because most of these laws/Acts were included in the Ninth Schedule of the Constitution of India before the decision in the Kesavananda Bharati case.

Article 31A (2) provides constitutional protection to tenure holders, i.e. bargadars or as sharecroppers. Thus, Article 31A covers most of the tenure holdings including rights all types of land, viz. waste land, forest land, land for pasture, sites of buildings occupied by cultivators, agricultural labourers and village artisans.

The Supreme Court has consistently held that there is a public purpose where the property is taken over to keep labour going on and contended and to maintain supply of essential commodities.

Comments: After the judgment in Kesavandana Bharti case, the Supreme Court has been testing Acts or statutes, put under the umbrella of IXth Schedule of the Constitution whether they violate the basic feature of the Constitution. This touchstone is sometime risky as land is a very complicated subject which is within the ambit of the State Governments except land acquisition. In Ratnagiri Engineering Pvt. Ltd. Case / [(2009) 456 CC 453)] the Supreme Court allowed the conversion of land from the industrial classification to the real estate purpose invalidating relevant provision of the West Bengal Estate Acquisition Act, 1953. The State Government has passed the law invalidating the judgment of the Supreme Court in this case. It is hoped that the Supreme Court will adopt a visionary instance to protect the rights of landless and the sharecroppers who are the backbone of the agriculture in the country as the Apex Court had been doing in the past before the Kesavananda Bharati case. At the same time State Governments and Union of India will ensure that there is no indiscriminate inclusion of statute or Act in the IXth Schedule of the Constitution without adequate public purpose.

44

Pune Municipal Corporation and Anr. vs Harakchand Misirimal Solanki and Ors.

(2014) 3 SCC 183

Deposit of compensation for land acquisition in treasury is not payment.

Fact: 18 appeals by special leave were filed by the landowners. It is argued on behalf of the landowners that in view of Section 24(2) of The Right to Fair Compensation and Transparency in Land Acquisition, Rehabilitation and Resettlement Act, 2013 (for short, '2013 Act'), the subject land acquisition proceedings initiated under the Land Acquisition Act, 1894 (for short, '1894 Act') have lapsed. The question for decision relates to true meaning of the expression: "compensation has not been paid" occurring in Section 24(2) of the 2013 Act.

Decision: The state depositing the compensation in its own treasury cannot be equated with the landowners being "paid". In exceptional circumstances, where the landowner refuses the compensation, the sum can be deposited with the court, but a deposit in its own treasury would not suffice. In other words, land acquisition proceedings under the 1894 Act will lapse.

45

Indore Development Authority vs Manoharlal and Ors.
(2020) SCC Online SC 316

Non-deposit of compensation in court does not amount to lapse of proceeding of land acquisition.

Fact: This Pune Municipal reasoning was held for nearly over three years, until a two judges bench comprising Justice Arun Mishra and Amitava Roy doubted its correctness in the Indore Development Authority case in December 2017 and referred it to larger bench. The three-judge bench (by 2:1 majority) held the decision in Pune Municipal Corporation to be per incuriam. While Justices Arun Mishra and A K Goel were in the majority, Justice Mohan M Shantanagoudar dissented by stating that a three-judge bench cannot overrule a precedent laid down by a co-ordinate bench. Shortly, another three-judge bench (Justices Madan B Lokur, Kurian Joseph and Deepak Gupta) took objection to this course adopted by Justice Arun Mishra-led bench in the Indore Development Authority case, and stayed the operation of Indore Development Authority case. It was only after this that a two-judge bench headed by Justice Arun Mishra thought it fit to refer the issue to the CJI for determination by a larger bench.

Decision: The Bench unanimously held that the land owners who had refused to accept compensation or who sought reference for higher compensation, cannot claim that the acquisition proceedings had lapsed under Section 24(2) of the Right to Fair Compensation and Transparency in Land Acquisition, Rehabilitation and Resettlement Act, 2013 (Land Acquisition Act, 2013). Once the compensation amount is tendered in the treasury, the state's obligation is complete with respect to the payment of compensation. The deemed lapse was intended to benefit landowners who could be allowed to claim lapse of proceedings which were initiated under the 1894 Act so that they could be subject to the more favourable proceedings under the 2013 Act. The expression paid in the main part of Section 24(2) of the Act of 2013 does not include a deposit of compensation in court....Non-deposit of compensation (in court) does not result in the lapse of land acquisition proceedings. The bench therefore, concluded that landowners, who had refused to accept the compensation under the earlier Act, cannot take benefit of deemed lapse of acquisition under Section 24 of the new Act of 2013.

46

Vellore Citizens' Welfare Forum vs UOI

1996 AIR 2715 = (1996) 5 SCC 647

Polluters should pay.

The Supreme Court in this case gave the landmark decision where it introduced the two internationally recognized principles on environment law in Indian Judicial system, i.e., Polluters Pay Principle and Precautionary Principle.

Facts: Vellore Citizens "Welfare Forum filed a PIL against the tanneries and other industries in the State of Tamil Nadu as they caused pollution by discharging the untreated effluent into the waterbodies and road side. These water bodies were the main source of water supply to the residents of the area.

Decision: Holding the tanneries and industries liable for their actions the court stated that while industries are vital for country's development, however they cannot be allowed to cause environmental pollution. The court stated that every citizen has right to a pollution-free environment. The root of such right is enshrined in the principle of Sustainable Development. Sustainable Development means "Development that meets the needs of the present without compromising the ability of the future generations to meet their own needs". It further observed that "precautionary principle" and "polluter pays principle" are essential components of the principle of "sustainable development". "Precautionary principle" means various measures taken by to be taken by the state Government and the concerned authorities to anticipate, prevent and attack the causes of environmental degradation. The principle of "polluter pays" means that one who carries on a hazardous activity is liable to make good the loss caused to another person by such activity. Before this judgement these two principles did not form part of Indian Jurisprudence but in this case, the court stated that right to clean environment was part of Right To Life as given under Article 21.

47

Indian Young Lawyer's Association & Others vs State of Kerala & Others (Sabrimala Temple Entry Case) (2019) 17 SCC 1

Women can not be prohibited to enter into the temples.

Facts: Sabrimala Temple Entry Case is about the conflict between women rights and tradition. The issue traces its origin to a 1991 case where an advocate had challenged the then Kerala government's decision to allow the entry of women inside the temple of Lord Ayappa. The division bench of Kerala High court in this case upheld the entry ban stating that the practice is prevalent from time immemorial. The high court further held that only the chief priest was empowered to decide on traditions. After the court's verdict the entry for the women inside the temple was again prohibited.

It was not until 2006 when this ban was again challenged in the court on the constitutional grounds. The petitioners in this case sought the court to declare the rule 3(b) of the Kerala Hindu places of public worship (authorization of Entry rules) 1965, unconstitutional as it restricts the entry of women into the Sabrimala Temple.

Decision: A 5 judge bench of honorable Supreme Court ruled 4 is to 1 in favor of allowing women of all ages to enter the temple. Chief Justice Dipak Misra, Justice RF Nariman, Justice AM Khanwilkar and Justice DY Chandrachud formed the majority, while the lone woman judge on the Bench, Justice Indu Malhotra dissented.

The court in its majority judgement stated that the practice of prohibiting the entry of women inside the temple was discriminatory in nature and that it violated Hindu women's constitutional right to pray and practice religion. It further stated that prohibition on grounds of biological and physiological features like menstruation amounted to discrimination based on gender and hence it violates right to equality (Art.14 of Constitution) of women.

48

Rustom Cavasjee Cooper vs Union of India

AIR 1970 SC 564 = 1970 (1) SCC 248

Nationalisation of Banks was declared invalid.

Facts: About 14 commercial banks were nationalised in 1969. Before undertaking this drastic step by enacting Banking Companies (Acquisitions and Transfer of Undertakings) Act, 22 of 1969 there was a controversy whether the purposes for which banks should be nationalised could better be achieved by what was called social control over banks by the exercise of powers vested in the Govt. of India under the Banking Regulation Act. Social control over banks meant issuing of such regulations and directions as may be necessary for implementing the legislations made for social good such as providing credit to the business and agriculture on liberal terms in association with the Govt. of India. This conflict generated heated debate in public and accordingly the Banking Companies (Acquisition & Transfer of Undertakings) Act 22 of 1969 has come to be questioned on all possible grounds. None of those grounds survive today because Art. 31 of the Constitution which relates to right to property has since been repealed. The question however as to how the matter relating to compensation was viewed at that time can be found in these judgments.

Decision: The broad object underlying the principle of valuation is to award to the owner the equivalent of his property with its existing advantages and its potentialities. Where there is an established market for the property acquired the problem of valuation presents little difficulty. Where there is no established market for the property, the object of the principle of valuation must be to pay to the owner for what he has lost, including the benefit of advantages present as well as future, without taking into account the urgency of acquisition, the disinclination of the owner to part with the property, and the benefit which the acquirer is likely to obtain by the acquisition. Under the Land Acquisition Acts compensation paid is the value to the owner together with all its potentialities and its special adaptability if the land is peculiarly suitable for a particular use, if it gives an enhanced value at the date of acquisition.

The important methods of determination of compensation are— (i) market value determined from sales of comparable properties, proximate in time to the date of acquisition, similarly situate, and possessing the same or similar advantages and subject to the same or similar disadvantages. Market value is the price the property may fetch in the open market if sold by a willing seller unaffected by the special needs of a particular purchase; (ii) capitalization of the net annual profit out of the property at a rate equal in normal cases to the return from gilt-edged securities. Ordinarily value of the property may be determined by capitalizing the net annual value obtainable in the market at the date of the notice of acquisition, (iii) where the property is a house, expenditure likely to be incurred for constructing a similar house, and reduced by the depreciation for the number of years since it was constructed; (iv) principle of reinstatement, where it is satisfactorily established that reinstatement in some other place is *bona fide* intended, there being no general market for the property for the purpose for which it is devoted (the purpose being a public purpose) and would have continued to be devoted, but for compulsory acquisition. Here compensation will be assessed on the basis of reasonable cost of reinstatement; (v) when the property has outgrown its utility and it is reasonably incapable of economic use, it may be valued as land plus the breakup value of the structure. But the fact that the acquirer does not intend to use the property for which it is used at the time of acquisition and desires to demolish it or use it for other purpose is irrelevant; and (vi) the property to be acquired has ordinarily to be valued as a unit. Normally an aggregate of the value of different components will not be the value of the unit.

These are, however, not the only methods. The method of determining the value of property by the application of an appropriate multiplier to the net annual income or profit is a satisfactory method of valuation of lands with buildings, only if the land is fully developed, i.e., it has been put to full use legally permissible and economically justifiable, and the income out of the property is the normal commercial and not a controlled return or a return depreciated on account of special circumstances. If the property is not fully developed, or the return is not commercial the method may yield a misleading result."

Comment: In this context, Parliament by passing forward looking legislation made this decision/ruling ineffective and demonstrated its supermacy over the judiciary which is the well recognized law of the land till this date.

49

CPIO, Supreme Court vs Subhash Chandra Agarwal 2019 SCC Online SC 1459

Even office of Chief Justice of India comes under purview of RTI Act.

On an RTI request made by activist Subhash Chandra Agarwal, in 2009, the Central Information Commission (CIC) ordered the Supreme Court of India to divulge material regarding if Supreme Court justices had declared their assets to the Chief Justice of India. The Supreme Court appealed against this order to itself. The Supreme Court stayed the CIC order. The court then referred the matter to a five judge Constitution Bench. The Court concluded that the Court is a "public authority" as defined in Section 2(h) of the RTI Act and is hence obliged to entertain the RTI applications and deal with them on case to case basis, i.e. to weigh the scales and on balance determine whether information should be furnished or would be exempt.

The Supreme Court held that the office of the Chief Justice of India is a public authority under the transparency law, the Right to Information (RTI) Act.

The Constitution Bench upheld the the 2010 judgment of Delhi HC which had held that RTI Act was applicable to CJI's office.

"Transparency does not undermine judicial independence. Judicial independence and accountability go hand in hand. Disclosure is a facet of public interest."

Cautioning that RTI cannot be used as tool of surveillance, the top court held that judicial independence has to be kept in mind while dealing with transparency. It said that only names of judges recommended by the Collegium can be disclosed, not the reasons.

50

M. Siddiq vs Mahant Suresh Das (Babri Masjid Case) 2019 SCC Online SC 958

The disputed site belongs to the Hindus.

The Babri mosque was built around 1528-29 CE by Mir Baqi. According to the Hindu community that mosque was established by annihilating a temple which was also the birthplace of Lord Rama. The earliest clash over the control of the site was in the year 1853 when during the British Raj both Hindus and Muslims denied each other title over the land over the site. The Britishers gave to the Hindus the outer area and the Muslims were given the inner area. The matter reached the Allahbad High Court which divided the land among the parties. The appeal was made against the verdict. The honourable Supreme Court after a 40 days of case hearings and case proceedings came to a judgement.

The following points sum up the judgement given by the Supreme Court:

- The Muslims cannot assert the disputed property as they were never in the possession of the land.
- On the basis of ASI's findings where Hindu religious remains were unearthed from the site, it was confirmed that the land belonged to the Hindus.
- The disputed land of 2.77 acres was thus given to the Hindus to construct a temple. On the other hand, Muslims would be given 5 acres of land in Ayodhya at some prominent place to build a mosque.

Comments: The Judjment solved the long standing national dispute which was thwarting all other solutions. Credit goes, to the Apex Court and shows confidence reposed by people in the wisdom and decision of the Supreme Court.

51

Mohd. Ahmed Khan vs Shah Bano Begum

AIR 1979 SC 362

Right of maintenance of a Muslim woman. There is need for a uniform civil code.

Section 125 of CrPC does not discriminate. Rather, irrespective of religion, a woman could seek maintenance under section 125 CrPC.

Facts: Mohd. Ahmed Khan married Shah Bano Begum in 1932. Five children were born to them. In the year 1975, i.e., after 43 years of married life the husband threw away his wife out of his house. In April 1978, when she filed an application for maintenance under Section 125 Criminal Procedure Code, the husband came out with a reply that he had divorced his wife on 6th November, 1975 and hence he was not liable to pay maintenance to the divorced wife as per Muslim Law. However, the Magistrate ordered the husband for payment of maintenace at the rate of ₹25/- p.m. which was enhanced to ₹179.20 paise per month by the High Court of Madhya Pradesh after a revisional application filed by wife in July 1980, even thugh according to the statement of the wife that her husband as an Adovcate earned over ₹60,000/- per year. The appellant before the Supreme Court was the husband. According to his contention under the Muslim Law the liability of the husband to maintain divorced wife was limited to the period of *Iddat* and not beyond. In this appeal, it was urged that the earlier two judgments rendered by this Court in *Bai Tahera* and *Fazilubi* which held that notwithstanding personal law of Muslims Sec. 125 Criminal Procedure Code which is general law applies to all persons standing in relationship of husbadn and wife irrespective of the religion they profess. The Supreme court agreed for reconsideration but confirmed those judgments affirming that the divorced Muslim wife was entitled to maintenance against her husband.

The court after disapproving the submissions made by interveners including the Mulsim Peronal Law Board who supported the appellant and appreciating those who supported the divorced wife's claim for maintenance, recommended to the Government to take early steps to enact the common Civil Code.

It is also a matter of regret that Article 44 of our Constitution has remained a dead letter. It provides that "the State shall endeavour to secure for the citizens a uniform civil code throughout the territory of India". There is no evidence of any official activity for framing a common civil code for the country. A belief seems to have gained ground that it is for the Muslim community to take a lead in the matter of reforms of their personal law. A common Civil Code will help the cause of national integration by removing divided loyalties to laws which have conflicting ideologies. No community is likely to bell the cat by making gratuitous concessions on this issue. It is the State which is charged with the duty of securing a uniform civil code for the citizens of the country and, unquestionably, it has the legislative competence to do so. A counsel in the case whispered, somewhat audibly, that legislative competence is one thing, the political courage to use that competence is quite another. We understand the difficulties involved in bringing persons of different faiths and persuasions on a common platform. But, a beginning has to be made if the Constitution is to have any meaning. Inevitably, the role of the reformer has to be assumed by the courts because, it is beyond the endurance of sensitive minds to allow injustice to be suffered when it is so palpable. But piecemeal attempts of courts to bridge the gap between personal law cannot take the place of a common Civil Code. Justice to all is a far more satisfactory way of dispensing justice than justice from case to case.

Comment: Instead of taking steps for enacting a common Civil Code, the Government enacted a special legislation called Protection of Muslim Women on Divorce Act which dis-entitled the Muslim Divorced Women to claim maintenance from their husbands but can raise such claim for a charitable payment from Muslim Wakf Boards.

Later on, in the case Shayara Bano vs Union of India, the Supreme Court on August 22, 2017 by 3 : 2 majority held that the Triple Talaq practice was unconstitutional, as it violates Muslim women's right to equality among other constitutional freedom. It is manifestly arbitrary in nature. (2017, 9 SCC 1 (SC)).

52

Anuradha Bhasin vs Union of India and Ors.

2020 SCC Online SC 25

Freedom of Internet can not be curtailed.

The Hon'ble Supreme Court of India vide its Judgment in the matter of Anuradha Bhasin vs Union of India and Ors. dated January 10, 2020 has held that freedom of speech and expression through the medium of internet is a fundamental right.

The Hon'ble Supreme Court held that the freedom of speech and expression through the medium of internet is a fundamental right under Article 19(1)(a) of the Constitution. Further, it also stated that the restrictions on internet have to follow the principles of proportionality under Article 19(2) of the Constitution. Further, it has banned the suspension of internet for indefinite period. It has also clarified that the prohibitory orders under Section 144 of Criminal Procedure Code cannot be imposed to suppress legitimate expression of opinion or grievance or exercise of any democratic rights.

The Hon'ble Supreme Court vide Judgment has held that freedom of speech and expression and freedom of trade and commerce through internet is also constitutionally protected right under Article 19(1)(g).

Part IV: Directive Principles of State Policy

Articles 36-51 cover Directive Principles of State Policy. These are some of the features that were considered to be fundamental to the governance of the country. The makers of the Constitution intended them to be the guiding principles for the government in power with regard to matters concerning the administration and governance. They enshrine a wide range of ideologies. Some of the directive principles such as organization of village panchayat and abolition of cow slaughter reflect Gandhian values and directive principles such as distribution of ownership and control of the material resources of the community reflect the socialist principles. However, the catch with respect to Directive Principles is that they are non-justiciable (Article 37). This means that there would lie no remedy for their violation in a court of law. Although they are non-justiciable, many of them have been upheld as integral part of the Constitution in several cases. For e.g. in the case of *Hussainara Khatoon vs State of Bihar* the Supreme Court held right to free and legal aid, provided under Article 39A as a fundamental right. In the same way, the Directive Principle of 'Separation of executive from judiciary' has been held to be part of the basic structure of the Constitution.

53

State of Kerala vs N.M. Thomas (1976) 2SCC 310

Harmonious reading of Part Three and Part Four of the Constitution.

In this case, the constitutionality of a government order that granted provisional promotions to employees belonging to the SC and ST category who did not possess the required qualifications and were given a two year time period to obtain the required qualification, was challenged in the Supreme Court. Court, reading harmoniously Article 46 with Article 16, held that order to be valid.

The Directive Principles of State Policy as a system frame-work values that gave life to the abstract concept outlined in the fundamental rights chapter. It was the Directive Principles that provided the justification for why the constitutional vision of equality was senstive to group disadvantage. This ruling made the static elements of Directive Principles of State Policy as dynamic ones.

54

MC Mehta vs Union of India (1982) 4 SCC 483 and 1988 SCC 471

Ganga cleaning should be ensured.

Facts:

- Due to discharge of untreated effluents in the Ganga river, the water of the river was rendered unsafe for drinking, fishing and bathing purposes, essentially creating a public nuisance.
- In 1985, M.C. Mehta filed a writ petition in the nature of mandamus to prevent these leather tanneries from disposing off domestic and industrial waste and effluents in the Ganga river. This writ petition was bifurcated by the Supreme Court into two parts known as Mehta I and Mehta II.

Decision:

- It is the responsibility of industries to treat their trade wastes in such a way that they do not deteriorate the quality of the receiving waters, which otherwise would make the utilisation of such polluted waters very difficult or costly for downstream settlers. The Nagar Mahapalika of Kanpur had to bear the major responsibility for the pollution of the river near the Kanpur city.
- The nuisance caused by the pollution of the river Ganga is a public nuisance, which is wide spread in range and indiscriminate in its effect and it would not be reasonable to expect any particular person lo take proceedings to stop it as distinct from the community at large.
- Kanpur Nagar Mahapalika was ordered to increase the size of sewers in the labour colonies and increase the number of public latrines and urinals for the use of poor people. The Court further held that the financial capacity of the

tanneries should be considered as irrelevant while requiring them to establish primary treatment plants.

- The Court highlighted the importance of certain provisions in our constitutional framework which enshrine the importance and the need for protecting our environment. Article 48-A provides that the State shall endeavor to protect and improve the environment and to safeguard the forests and wild life of the country. Article 51-A of the Constitution of India, imposes a fundamental duty on every citizen to protect and improve the natural environment including forests, lakes, rivers and wild life.
- The Court stated the importance of the Water (Prevention and Control of Pollution) Act, 1974 ('the Water Act'). This Act was passed to prevent and control water pollution and maintaining water quality. This Act established central and state boards and conferred them with power and functions relating to the control and prevention of water pollution.

Comments: The State should arrange for prevention of pollution in the river Ganga and other water-sources. The judgment gave fillip to the constitution of the Central Ganga Authority under the Prime Minister to clean the river Ganges and other rivers in the country.

55

Indian Council of Enviro-legal Action, Petitioner and Union of India and Others, Respondents

AIR 1996 SC 1446 = 1996 (3) SCC 212

Polluter pays and shall pay himself.

Facts: Concerned with the environmental degradation and consequent misery the people had been suffering on account of the absolute neglect of the measures they should take to protect environment, by the chemical industries, the petitioner who was a public service body, approached the Supreme Court for directions to the offending industries to shift their establishments to distant places, to remove the damaging material causing health hazards to the local people and also to pay compensation to all those affected by chemical pollution.

The Supreme Court upheld the petitioner's submissions and confirmed as rule of law the principles that the polluter shall bear and pay himself all the costs of shifting the industries as well as all the costs required for remedial measures. The polluter shall also pay compensation to all those who were affected by pollution.

The Court observed that Environment Protection Act confers on the Central Government the power to give directions of the above nature and to the above effect (i.e. to direct the polluter to take up all remedial measures) levying of the costs required for carrying out remedial measures is implicit in Sections 3 and 4 of Environment Protection Act which sections are couched in very wide language. Therefore, appropriate directions can be given by this Court to the Central Government to invoke and exercise those powers.

Decision: The question of liability of the respondents to defray the costs of remedial measures can also be looked into from another angle, which has now come to be accepted universally as a sound principle, viz., the "Polluter Pays" Principle.

The polluter pays principle demands that the financial costs of preventing or remedying damage caused by pollution should lie with the undertakings which cause the pollution, or produce the goods which cause the pollution. Under the principle it is not the role of Government to meet the costs involved in either prevention of such damage, or in carrying out remedial action, because the effect of this would be to shift the financial burden of the pollution incident to the taxpayer. The 'polluter pays' principle was promoted by the Organisation for Economic Co-operation and Development (OECD) during the 1970s when there was great public interest in environmental issues. During this time there were demands on Government and other institutions to introduce policies and mechanisms for the protection of the environment and the public from the threats posed by pollution in a modern industrialised society. Since then there has been considerable discussion of the nature of the polluter pays principle, but the precise scope of the principle and its implications for those involved in past, or potentially polluting activities have never been satisfactorily agreed.

Despite the difficulties inherent in defining the principle, the European Community accepted it as a fundamental part of its strategy on environmental matters, and it has been one of the underlying principles of the four Community Action Programmes on the Environment. The current Fourth Action Programme (1987) O.J. C 328/1) makes it clear that the cost of preventing and eliminating nuisances must in principle be borne by the polluter, and the polluter pays' principle has now been incorporated into the European Community Treaty as part of the new Articles on the environment which were introduced by the Single European Act of 1986. Article 120R (2) of the Treaty states that environmental considerations are to play a part in all the policies of the Community, and that action is to be based on three principles:

the need for preventive action: the need for environmental damage to be rectified at source; and that the polluter should pay.

("Historic Pollution—Does the Polluter pay?" By Carolyn Shelbourn—Journal of Planning and Environmental Law. August 1974 issue.)

Thus, according to this principle, the responsibility for repairing the damage is that of the offending industry. Sections 3 and 5 empower the Central Government to give directions and take measures for giving effect to this Principle. In all the circumstances of the case, we think it appropriate that the task of determining the amount required for carrying out the remedial measures, its recovery/realisation and the task of undertaking the remedial measures is placed upon the Central Government in the light of the provisions of the Environment (Protection) Act, 1986. It is, of course, open to the Central Government to take the help and assistance of State Government, R.P.C.B. or such other agency or authority, as they think fit.

56

M.C. Mehta, Petitioner, Union of India, Respondent

AIR 1999 SC 291 = 1998 (8) SCC 206

Ban on Transport Vehicles of more than 15 years old

Fact: Bhure Lal Committee recommended that transport vehicles which are more than 15 years old shall be banned from operating on public roads. Supreme Court has directed that all those vehicles which are more than 15 years old shall not be permitted to ply in the National Capital Territory of Delhi, with effect from 2nd October, 1998. Noticing that the said order is not being implemented, the Supreme Court by an order dated 22.9.1998 extended the period upto 31st December in a graded fashion.

Dicision: In the context of the existing vehicles which are running on the roads in the National Capital, the ages of which range from 21 years to more than 25 years, and noticing that the number of vehicles which are more than from 15 to 16 years old were 2962 and those ranging from 17 to 19 years are 3200 and those which are above 19 years upto 25 years were 9349, Court modified the earlier order which fixed the date of which they should be withdrawn on 1st October, 1998, modified order and directed that:

(a) that all commercial/transport vehicles which are more than 20 years old (9349) shall be phased out and not permitted to ply in the National Capital Territory, Delhi after 2nd October, 1998;

(b) all such commercial/transport vehicles which are 17 to 19 years old (3200) shall not be permitted to ply after 15th November, 1998;

(c) such commercial/transport vehicles which are 15 years and 16 years old (4962) shall not be permitted to ply after 31st December, 1998.

This order shall apply to all commercial/transport vehicles whether registered in the National Capital Territory of Delhi or outside (but ply in Delhi) which are more than the stipulated age.

This ban order shall also be applicable to all such vehicles which do not have any authority or permit to ply in the National Capital Territory of Delhi.

Apart from the commercial/transport vehicles which are registered as noticed above, we are informed that there are vehicles which are either not registered or on which road tax has not been paid in the National Capital Territory of Delhi. We direct that all such commercial/transport vehicles which are being plied without payment of road tax or registration shall not be allowed to ply in the National Capital Territory forthwith and in any event not with effect from 2nd October, 1998.

Comment: In this case, after the Supreme Court has issued its first set of directions on the question of imposing a total ban on plying of the vehicles in public roads, aged more than 15 years. There were widespread protests not only from the operators but also from the public which include commuters and school going children. In response to the same, the Supreme Court modified its directions to enable the administration to implement the orders of the Court in a phased and graded manner.

57

Supreme Court Advocates on Record vs Union of India 1993 (4) SCC 441

The collegium system in the Supreme Court for appointment and transfer of judges is restored.

Facts:

- In 2015, the Supreme Court Advocates-On-Record Association and Senior Advocates filed writ petitions before the Supreme Court challenging the constitutionality of the Ninety-Ninth (99th) amendment of the Constitution and the NJAC Act, 2015. The petitions alleged, inter alia, that the NJAC violated the basic structure of the Constitution by compromising the judiciary's independence.
- In 2014 the NDA government introduced the Constitution (121st Amendment) Bill, which was subsequently passed by both houses of the parliament, ratified by 16 state legislatures and assented by the President; NJAC Act and the Constitutional Amendment Act came into force from 13 April 2015.

Decision:

- The collegium system for appointment and transfer of judges was restored. The court has struck down The Constitution (Ninety-ninth Amendment) Act, 2014 and The National Judicial Appointments Commission Act, 2014, declaring them to be unconstitutional and void with a majority of 4:1.
- The Court held that the Constitution mandates judicial primacy in appointments concerning the judiciary. Based on the constitutional text and longstanding practice, the Court held that judicial primacy is not only constitutionally required, but is also part of the unamendable basic structure because it is integral to the independence of the

judiciary. Thus, as a consequence, the NJAC was held unconstitutional for violating the requirements of judicial primacy and judicial independence.

- The term 'independence of judiciary' culminates from a collective reading of Article 12, 36 and 50. It is sometimes not possible, to deduce the concerned "basic structure" from a plain reading of the provisions of the Constitution. Therefore, when a plea is advanced raising a challenge on the basis of the violation of the "basic structure with reference to the "independence of the judiciary" its rightful understanding is, and has to be, that Articles 12, 36 and 50 on the one hand, and Articles 124, 217 and 222 on the other.

Comments: This ruling gave due autonomy and independence to the judiciary making the apex court as watchdog over the state activities.

Part V: Elections

This part only consists of five Articles, from Article 324 to Article 329. Different Articles deal with different aspects of elections and procedures related to them.

Article 324 states that 'superintendence, direction and control of the elections are to be vested in an election commission'. The election commission consists of a 'chief election commissioner' and such other number of election commissioners as the President may from time to time fix. The objective of the constituent assembly behind enacting this Article was to ensure the independence of the Election Commission. While enacting this Article, Dr. B.R. Ambedkar said, 'the whole election machinery shall be in the hands of a central election commission'.

In the case of *Mohinder Singh Gill & Anr. vs The Chief Election Commissioner, New Delhi and Ors (1977)* held that the Article 324 comes into operation over matters relating to election where legislation does not exist and there lies a wide discretion with respect to exercise of power and duties. Such powers and duties can be either legislative, administrative or even adjudicative. The Constitution does not define the area of operation of Article 324 exhaustively. It vests the entire power and responsibility with respect to conduct of national and state elections in the Election Commission. Hence the discretionary powers of the ECI are very vast. However, the power is not to be exercised maliciously, mindlessly or arbitrarily.

58

Public Interest Foundation vs Union of India

W.P. (C) 536/2011, 2018 Latest Case Law 706 SC

Candidates and political party shall make declaration about the candidate's history.

Facts:

- In 2011, the Public Interest Foundation, a NGO, filed a writ petition in the Supreme Court to expand the grounds for disqualification of membership in Parliament/State Legislatures, under Article 32 of the Constitution. They asked the Court to disqualify candidates and legislators under the Representation of Peoples Act, 1951 (RP Act), who have serious criminal charges framed against them by a court. In addition, they asked the Court to disqualify candidates, who file false affidavits.
- On 8th March 2016, a Division Bench of three-judges referred the matter to be heard by a Constitution Bench. This Bench rejected the Union's argument that these questions were already settled by the Constitution Bench in Manoj Narula case in 2014. In Manoj Narula, the court chose not to interfere with the Prime Minister's discretion to choose Ministers, even though some Ministers may be undertrials in pending criminal cases.

Decision:

- The Bench delivered its verdict and declined to add further criteria for disqualification under Section 8 of the RP Act, observing that it was not for the Courts but the Legislature to bring about changes to the law. It further urged the Parliament to enact law to ensure that persons facing serious criminal charges were prevented from entering the political stream.

- The Five - Judges of the Constitution Bench ruled that candidates should not be excluded solely because they were convicted in a criminal case. The bench also advised the legislature to consider changing the legislation to facilitate the decriminalization of politics. The Court further held that candidate must fill out the form as given by the Election Commission and the form must contain all the information as needed. The form must state in bold letters, in recognition of the criminal proceedings pending against the nominee. When a candidate seeks an election on the ticket of a specific party, he/she is expected to notify the party of the criminal proceedings pending against him/her. The political party concerned shall be obligated to make available on its website the details referred to above concerning candidates with a criminal record. Both the candidate and the political party concerned shall make a declaration in the widely circulated local newspapers about the candidate's history and shall also make a large publicity in the electronic media.

Part VI: Power and Role of President

To better understand the Constitutional position of President, Articles 53, 74 and 75 shall be referred to. Article 53 states that the executive power of the Union shall be exercised by the President in accordance with the provisions of the Constitution. Article 74 provides for a council of minister to aid and advise the President. The President 'shall' act in accordance with such advice while exercising his functions. This means that the President is bound by the advice of Council of Ministers, which is to be led by a Prime Minister. Article 75(1) provides that the prime minister is to be appointed by the president and other minsters of his cabinet are also to be appointed by the President but on the advice of Prime Minister. From these provisions it becomes clear that the President is only the Constitutional head whereas the real power vests with the council of minister headed by a Prime Minster. In *Ram Jawaya Kapur vs State of Punjab (1955)* the bench stated that the President is only the Constitutional head of the executive while the real power vests with the Council of Ministers commanded by a Prime Minister.

The collective responsibility of the council of ministers further makes President a figure head. But President can exercise his discretion in many critical situations like proclamation of emergency or imposition of the President Rule in the state. Thus, there are two loci in which people of India have faith.

59

U.N.R Rao vs Indira Gandhi (1971) 2 SCC 635 = AIR 1971 SC 1002

P.M. and her cabinet continue to aid and advise the President even after dissolution of Parliament.

Facts: After the Congress party split in two factions in 1969, Indira Gandhi, the then Prime Minister advised the President to dissolve the Lok Sabha in accordance with the exercise of his powers given under Article 85 (2) (b). Her motive was to conduct fresh general elections in the country so that all the doubts that exist with respect to her leadership could be assailed. The President acted according to her advice and dissolved the lower house of the parliament or Lok Sabha. However, despite the dissolution of the house, Smt. Indira Gandhi continued to act as the Prime Minister. U.N.R Rao, an advocate at Madras High Court, challenged before the Supreme Court the continuance of Smt. Gandhi as the Prime Minister. His primary contention that once the lower house is dissolved then the council of ministers (consisting prime minister and minsters appointed on his advice) shall also resign. He based his argument upon Article 75(3) which says that the council of ministers shall be collectively to the House of People. Hence, the question arose that if the house has been dissolved then how can the Council of Ministers (including the Prime Minister) continue to occupy their earlier positions.

Issue: Can the council of ministers continue even after the dissolution of the lower house?

Decision: The court drew a parallel with the system that exists in England. In England, even when the lower house is dissolved the cabinet led by Prime Minister, continues to exist in order to ensure the smooth administration of the nation. The court also stated that Article 74 provides for a council of minister to aid and advise the President. The use of the word 'shall' in Article 74 (1) makes the requirement of council of minister to aid and advise the President to exercise his executive power 'a must' (a mandatory provision). Therefore, the petition was rejected and continuance of Smt. Gandhi and her cabinet at their positions even after the dissolution was upheld as Constitutionally valid.

60

S.P. Anand vs H.D. Deve Gowda AIR 1997 SC 271

Even non-member of the House can hold office for six months.

Facts: In the general elections of the year 1996, no party or alliance of parties could secure majority to form government. Ultimately United Front, with support of the Congress party managed to form the government. They surprisingly chose Sh. H.D. Deve Gowda, who was not a member of the Parliament, to be the Prime Minister. His election was challenged before the Supreme Court.

Issue: Is a non-member of Parliament eligible to be elected P.M.?

Decision: The court upheld Deve Gowda's appointment as P.M. It observed that Article 75(5) clearly states that a minister who is not elected to either house of parliament has six months' time to be get elected to either of the houses of the Parliament. At the expiration of such 6 months if the person fails to get elected, he/she also cease to be a minister. The word minister includes Prime Minster too. There's no distinction between the two as all the ministers are collectively responsible to the lower house of parliament or Lok Sabha. It finally held that as long as H.D. Deve Gowda enjoyed confidence of the house and fulfilled the requirement of Article 75(5), he is eligible to be elected P.M.

Power and Role of Governor

Article 153 states that there shall be a 'Governor' for each state. Article 154 states that the executive power of a state shall vest in the governor and shall be exercised by him through officers subordinate to him. Hence a Governor is the Constitutional head of a state, in the same way President is the Constitutional head of the Union. Provisions stating the extent of power and role of the governor are contained in Articles 153-162.

Part VII: Imposition of Emergency Under Article 356

356. (1) If the President, on receipt of a report from the Governor 1*** of a State or otherwise, is satisfied that a situation has arisen in which the Government of the State cannot be carried on in accordance with the provisions of this Constitution, the President may by Proclamation— (a) assume to himself all or any of the functions of the Government of the State and all or any of the powers vested in or exercisable by the Governor 2*** or anybody or authority in the State other than the Legislature of the State; (b) declare that the powers of the Legislature of the State shall be exercisable by or under the authority of Parliament; (c) make such incidental and consequential provisions as appear to the President to be necessary or desirable for giving effect to the objects of the Proclamation, including provisions for suspending in whole or in part the operation of any provisions of this Constitution relating to anybody or authority in the State.

The most controversial role of the President and the Governor in the Constitution is found in Article 356. Clause 1 of Article 356 provides that the President may impose Emergency, or Presidential Rule in a state based on the report of the Governor. Hence Governor and President play a vital role in imposition of emergency in a state. The extent and limits of their power and their roles under Article 356 has been widely discussed by the Supreme Court in several of its judgment. Two of the most landmark of those judgments are discussed hereafter.

61

S.R. Bommai vs Union of India AIR 1994 SC 1918

Before imposing the President Rule in the State, floor test should be conducted.

Facts: In 1989, when the then chief minister of the state of Karnataka, S.R. Bommai expanded his cabinet, many of his party members were dissatisfied. Soon several of those dissatisfied members defected. Mr. Bommai advised the Governor to exercise his power under Article 174 and call a session of the house so that a floor test could be done to test the majority. But the Governor did not pay heed to his advice and instead asked President to impose President's rule in the state in accordance with Article 356 (1). Acting on the Governor's advice, the President imposed emergency in the state. It was challenged by S.R. Bommai in the High Court. The court ruled that the grounds on which President forms decision to impose emergency in a state are open to judicial review. However, the High Court refused to declare the proclamation of emergency unconstitutional. Bommai decided to go to Supreme Court in appeal against this decision. At this same time, President's rule was imposed in three more states- Madhya Pradesh, Himachal Pradesh and Rajasthan on the grounds of failure of Constitutional machinery in the wake of riots that followed in these states after the Babri Masjid demolition. The court clubbed all these cases together and formed a nine-judge bench to decide the cases.

Decision: In this case, the court made certain observations with regard to imposition of President's rule under Article 356. Some of them are as follows-

(a) The Governor shall first conduct a floor tests before coming to the conclusion that no party enjoys majority in the house.

Only after conducting the floor test, if no party is able claim majority then the recommendation may be made by the Governor to the President to impose emergency.

(b) Though the advice tendered by the Governor to the President is protected from judicial review under Article 361 but the material on which such advice is based can be examined by the court on the grounds such as mala fide, arbitrariness, irrelevancy, etc.

(c) The President shall wisely exercise his/her discretion on imposing emergency after receiving report for the same by the governor.

(d) Governor shall display impartiality and non-partisanship.

62

Rameshwar Prasad vs Union of India AIR 2006 SC 980

Role of Governor comes into play after defection has taken place.

Facts: In 2004, the UPA led by Congress party, formed government at the centre. The 2005 Bihar Assembly had given a fractured mandate to the contesting parties which resulted in a hung assembly. The then Governor of Bihar, Buta Singh came to the conclusions that no party could claim majority in the state. He wrote to the president recommending him to impose President's rule in the state. The President acting on his advice suspended (but not dissolved) the state assembly and imposed president rule in the state. Meanwhile the parties started political realignment to claim majority in the State Assembly. National Democratic Alliance, led by BJP came close to securing majority in the assembly. Before NDA could move to Governor Office to claim majority, Governor Buta Singh sent two reports to President stating that instances of horse-trading taking place in the state. He recommended to the President to suspend the assembly and order fresh elections. The President accepted the recommendations and ordered fresh elections. This proclamation was challenged in the Supreme Court.

The challenge in these petitions is about constitutional validity of Notification dated 23.05.2005 ordering dissolution of the Legislative Assembly of Bihar on the ground that attempts are being made to cobble a majority by illegal means and lay claim to form the Government in the State and if these attempts continue, it would amount to tampering with constitutional provisions. The question before the Court was whether the dissolution of the Assembly under Article 356(1) of the Constitution could be ordered on the said ground. Linked with this question was the correctness of the dissolution even before the Assembly met for the first time after its due constitution and the members took oath.

Decision: It was argued before the court by the petitioners that since the first meeting of the assembly has not taken place, hence it cannot be dissolved. The Supreme Court rejected this argument. The court nevertheless declared the decision unconstitutional. It stated that the governor's report on which the decision for dissolution of assembly was made lacked any credible information to come to such conclusion. The court also made the observation that a governor's role is limited to ascertaining that whether a political or alliance can form government or not. As far as ensuring transparency in the electoral process is concerned, this is a task best left to the Election Commission.

The majority held that no such power has been vested with the governor as it would be against the democratic principles of the majority rule. The consequences can be horrendous and would open a floodgate of dissolution and will have far reaching alarming and dangerous consequences. It may also be a handle to reject post-election alignments and realignments on the ground of same being unethical plunging the country or the state into another election. It further held that there was no material, let alone relevant, with the governor to recommend dissolution and the drastic and extreme action of dissolution cannot be justified on mere ipse dixit, suspicion whims and facies of the governor. The Governor must not be allowed to take the plea that no government could be formed, unless he exhausts all possible options, including the one of asking the House itself to elect its Leader. Extreme step of imposition of President's Rule was nothing short of contempt of the electoral exercise and the verdict of the people. Moreover, the argument of so-called horse trading as stated in the Governor Report is most untenable because for dealing with horse trading and defections, it is the speaker under the 10th Schedule of the Constitution and the governor cannot usurp these functions. Even under 10th Schedule, the law comes into play only after the defection has taken place and not at the prospect or threat of defection.

Part VIII: Parliamentary Privileges

Articles 105 and 194 mention the privileges that are available to the Member of Parliament and to the members of state assembly, respectively. These privileges give them protection from any proceeding or suit against anything said or vote given by them in the Parliament. However, the extent of these privileges are not defined in the Constitution, i.e., Article 194 (3) of the Constitution states that the Power, Privileges and Immunities of a House of the State Legislature (Legislative Assembly and Legislative Council) shall be defined by the legislature through a law, and until such law is made the Power, Privileges and Immunities of a House of the State Legislature shall be same as those of the House of Commons of the United Kingdom. However, since no law has been formulated that would clearly define the extent of such privileges, the court relies on the interpretation of the Power, Privileges and Immunities of the House of Commons of the United Kingdom to determine the same for Parliament and the state legislatures.

63

Shibu Soren vs Dayanand Sahay and Ors.

(2001) 7 SCC 425

Office of profit of M.P. is defined.

Facts: Appellant secured the highest number of votes and was declared elected for the Rajya Sabha elections. Respondent No.1 was defeated, and filed an Election Petition on the ground that at the time of filling his nomination papers, the appellant was holding "an office of profit" under the State Government as Chairman of the Interim Jharkhand Area Autonomous Council ('JAAC'), and was thus disqualified to contest election. Appellant asserted that office of Chairman of the interim JAAC was not an 'office of profit' or even an 'office' under the State Government and the election petitioner was barred from raising the challenge, for not having raised that objection at the time of scrutiny of nomination papers before the returning officer. He was drawing only honorarium and allowances to meet his 'out of pocket expenses'. According to an additional plea raised by the appellant, his disqualification, if any stood removed by the Parliament (Prevention of Disqualification) Act, 1959 since he enjoyed the status of a Minister while functioning as Chairman of the Interim Council. Patna High Court allowed the petition and set aside election of the appellant. This appeal is directed against that judgment of the Patna High Court dated 19th May, 2000.

Decision: The three aspects - 'office', 'of profit, and 'under government' came up for decision before apex court in this case. The Supreme Court set aside the election of Shibu Soren, to Rajya Sabha, on the ground that he was holding "an office of profit" under the State Government as chairman of JAAC. The expression 'under government' was also explained: "with regard to the "office of profit", what needed to be found was, if the amount received by the person concerned from the office he/she holds provides some pecuniary gain, other than the compensation to defray him/her out of pocket expenses." The apex court held that Soren was holding office "at the pleasure of the State Government". The court noted that the government had the right to remove or dismiss the holder of that office, besides controlling the manner of functioning of the Interim Council and providing funds for the Interim Council, out of which an honorarium of Rs.1750 per month, besides daily allowance, rent-free accommodation and a chauffeur driven car at the state expense, was paid to the appellant. The CJI further observed that all this "was a benefit capable of bringing about a conflict between the duty and interest of the appellant as a Member of Parliament - the precise vice to which Article 102 (1)(a) is attracted".

64

P.V. Narsimha Rao vs State, (1998) 4 SCC 626

Bribe for giving vote inside Parliament is not covered.

Facts: In the General Election for 10th Lok Sabha (1991) Congress (I) party emerged as the single largest party and it formed the Government of P.V. Narasimha Rao. The support of 14 members was needed to have the no-confidence motion defeated. The no-confidence motion was lost. Certain members of the Lok Sabha having allegiance to the Jharkhand Mukti Morcha (the JMM), Janata Dal, and Ajit Singh group (the JD, AS) voted against the no-confidence motion. One Shri Ravindra Kumar filed a complaint on with the CBI, alleged that in July 1993 a criminal conspiracy was hatched pursuant to which the above members agreed to and did receive the bribes, to giving of which P.V. Narasimha Rao, MP and Prime Minister, along with others were parties to vote against the no-confidence motion. A prosecution was launched and cognizance was taken by the special Judge Delhi. The persons sought to be charged as aforesaid, filed petitions in the Delhi High Court seeking to quash the charges. The HC dismissed the petitions. Hence an appeal was filed in the Supreme Court of India.

Decision: Several parliamentarians were held immune from prosecution for bribery, as the alleged kickbacks were 'in respect of' a parliamentary vote, which are guarded by parliamentary immunity. However, in case of one of the accused, the Court denied immunity as he had not cast a vote, and made himself ineligible for parliamentary immunity, by delinking the relationship between his vote and alleged acceptance of bribe. The Court added "The immunity under clause (2) of Article

105 becomes available to a Member when he "makes a speech" or "gives his vote" in the parliamentary proceedings inside one of the Chambers of Parliament or in any committee thereof. Since the acts involving conspiracy and acceptance of bribe were wholly done by the accused outside the four walls of the legislative Chamber, it did not attract the immunity provision so as to protect them from criminal prosecution. Besides, these criminal acts themselves constitute completed crimes without reference to any goings on in Parliament and are capable of proof before the Special Judge independently of any proof or disproof of casting of vote by a Member in Parliament. Therefore, such offences could not be deemed to be acts "in respect of" the act of "giving of vote" inside Parliament."

Comment: This judgment can subsequently be reviewed.

65

Keshav Singh vs Speaker, Legislative Assembly AIR 1963 SC 745

Court can interfere in Parliamentary privilege as regards violation of fundamental rights if these are not codified.

In this case, the extent of Parliamentary Privileges and its position vis a vis other provisions of the Constitution, e.g., fundamental rights was discussed in this case.

Facts: In 1964, Keshav Singh, worker of Socialist Party in Gorakhpur, Uttar Pradesh, published a pamphlet along with two of his colleagues, against the local MLA of Gorakhpur accusing him of corruption and misappropriation of peoples' money. The state's legislative assembly took cognizance of his act and declared that it was violation of the immunities and privileges enjoyed by the MLAs as provided under Article 194 of the Constitution. He along with his colleagues was ordered by the assembly to appear before it in order to receive reprimand. Both of his colleagues acted accordingly and appeared before the assembly to receive the reprimand. However Keshav Singh refused to obey the orders citing lack of funds to make the journey from Gorakhpur to Lucknow (where the UP state assembly sits). This did not go down well with the assembly which ordered his arrest. He was later sentenced to jail for a week. Just one day before his release was due, his lawyer named Solomon, filed a petition before a two-judge bench of the High Court of Allahabad demanding his immediate release. His main argument was that the assembly did not give his client sufficient opportunity to answer the charges pressed against him. The government's counsel, who was required to put forward the government's side did not show up in the court on the day of hearing. The High Court ordered release of Keshav Singh on bail. The Speaker of State Assembly, called the granting of bail to Keshav Singh by the High Court an assault on the 'separation of powers' between the legislature, executive and judiciary. He was of the opinion that the court has undermined assembly's power to address an issue pertaining to breach of its privileges. On the basis of the observations made by the speaker, the assembly then passed a resolution against Keshav Singh's lawyer and the two judges who granted him bail holding all of them guilty of the breach assembly's privileges. The assembly ordered them to be taken into custody and be brought before it. The two judges who were ordered to be taken into custody by the assembly filed petition before the state High Court claiming that assembly's order violates the law laid down in Article 211 of the Constitution. Article 211 provides that no discussion shall take place in the legislature of the state with respect to the conduct of any judge of the Supreme Court or High Court in discharge of his/her duties. To display solidarity with the two judges and deter the state assembly from taking any action the future judges, the chief justice of Allahabad High Court formed a bench of all the judges of the High Court (which was 28 back then) to decide the matter. To this day, it remains the biggest bench ever constituted, either in High Court or the Supreme Court to hear any matter. As expected, the High Court unanimously put a stay on the arrest warrant of the two judges. The assembly, taking notice of the show of solidarity by the judges and to avoid any larger confrontation with the state judiciary altered its position. It withdrew the arrest warrant for the two judges. The matter soon grabbed the nation's attention. A Presidential reference under Article 143 was made by the then

Nehru Government to seek the Supreme Court's opinion on the whole matter.

Issue: What is the extent of the powers and privileges given to the Parliament and state legislative assemblies under the Constitution?

Decision: The Supreme Court formed a Constitutional bench of seven judges to hear this matter. To define the privileges of the state assembly it looked into the powers and privileges of the House of Commons of the U.K. Article 194 (3) of the Constitution states that the Power, Privileges and Immunities of a House of the State Legislature (Legislative Assembly and Legislative Council) shall be defined by the legislature through a law, and until such law is made the Power, Privileges and Immunities of a House of the State Legislature shall be same as those of the House of Commons of the United Kingdom. However, since no law has been formulated that would clearly define the extent of such privileges, the court relied on the interpretation of the Power, Privileges and Immunities of the House of Commons of the United Kingdom to determine the same for the state legislatures.

Also, Keshav Singh had raised contention before the Court that the exercise of privilege by the assembly violates his right to Personal Liberty given under Article 21. The court held that in such cases where there is a direct conflict between the right to exercise of parliamentary privileges and right to personal liberty, the latter shall prevail as rights given under Part Three of the Constitution are Fundamental Rights. This observation of the court was totally different from the court's previous ruling in the case of *M.S.M. Shrama vs Shri Krishna Sinha (1959)* where the court had discussed the interplay between the Fundamental Rights and Parliamentary Privileges. In that case, a newspaper had published an expunged part of the assembly's proceeding. Assembly issued a breach of privilege notice against the newspaper's editor. He argued in the court that the notice violates his fundamental right to Freedom of Speech and Expression. In that case the court held the Parliamentary Privileges to be supreme than any fundamental right.

Hence in the Kehsav Singh case, the court deviated from its position over 'conflict between the Parliamentary Privileges and Fundamental Rights' as enunciated in the MSM Sharma case.

The second question before the Court was the conflict between Article 211 and Parliamentary Privileges. The court held that in such cases law laid down in Article 211 of the Constitution shall prevail over Privileges. Article 211 provides that no discussion shall take place in the legislature of the state with respect to the conduct of any judge of the Supreme Court or High Court in discharge of his/her duties.

Comment: This decision of the Court was heavily criticized as it had technically declared Parliament to be subservient to judiciary when it comes to exercising the powers and privileges.

It is to be noted that till this date, Parliament has not codified its privileges and hence their lies a great scope for interpretation by the court.

Part IX: Miscellaneous Cases

Centre for Public Interest Litigation & Ors. vs Union of India & Ors. AIR 2012 SC 3725

Public auction is the best method for disposal of State owned natural resources-Spectrum case

Facts: While disposing of the 2G Spectrum in 2010, the Government of India followed the principle of first-come-first-served and adopted its price which was fixed in 2001. The action of the Government is questioned in the proceeding. The Court followed the view of the Controller and Auditor General of India and a new concept 'prospective losses'.

Decision: "There is a fundamental flaw in the first-come-first-served policy inasmuch as it involves an element of pure chance or accident. In matters involving award of contracts or grant of licence or permission to use public property, the invocation of first-come-first-served policy has inherently dangerous implications. Any person who has access to the power corridor at the highest or the lowest level may be able to obtain information from the Government files or the files of the agency/instrumentality of the State that a particular public property or asset is likely to be disposed of or a contract is likely to be awarded or a licence or permission is likely to be given, he would immediately make an application and would become entitled to stand first in the queue at the cost of all others who may have a better claim. This Court has repeatedly held that wherever a contract is to be awarded or a licence is to be given, the public authority must adopt a transparent and fair method for making selections so that all eligible persons get a fair opportunity of competition. To put it differently, the State and its agencies/instrumentalities must always adopt a rational method for disposal of public property and no attempt should be made to scuttle the claim of worthy applicants. When it comes to alienation of scarce natural resources like spectrum etc., it is the burden of the State to ensure that a non-discriminatory method is adopted for distribution and alienation, which would necessarily result in protection of national/public interest. In our view, a duly publicised auction conducted fairly and impartially is perhaps the best method for discharging this burden and the methods like first-come-first-served when used for alienation of natural resources/public property are likely to be misused by unscrupulous people who are only interested in garnering maximum financial benefit and have no respect for the constitutional ethos and values. In other words, while transferring or alienating the natural resources, the State is duly bound to adopt the method of auction by giving wide publicity so that all eligible persons can participate in thc process."

Comment: This is also a case in which the Supreme Court has interfered with the decisions of the executive and its policy. In this case, the executive has to decide not only the person to whom licence may be given but also his experience and the capacity. The executive, if necessary, shall wait till the candidate acquires the necessary finances and skill. The executive shall also see that the policy behind the disposal of natural resources is carried out successfully and not thwarted or frustrated. Neither the Controller and Auditor General, nor the Supreme Court can invoke the principle of "prospective losses' which has to be held necessarily as irrelevant to the policy of managing natural resources. The similar decision was held in the matter of auction of coal mines by Government of India and many civil servants including ministers are being prosecuted for violation of norms laid down by the Supreme Court in this case.

67

Parmanand Katra vs Union of India AIR 1989 SC (203)

Medical Care for Accident Victims

When an accident occurs on the road, some people hesitate to take the victims to a doctor or hospital as it would involve legal complications. The doctors also have some confusion about their primary duties when an accident victim is brought to them. Should the police be informed first? The police also create complications by raising objections to a particular clinic treating the victim. The accident occurred within one police station area and therefore the treatment should be given within that jurisdiction. Good Samaritans and doctors stand confused while the police quote the laws and rules till the victim dies of neglect. The present case deals with this problem. (The new Motor Vehicles Act 1988 has made it clear that it is medical care first and legal formalities later).

Facts: A lawyer, Parmanand Katra, of Delhi filed this public interest petition asking for a direction to the Central Government that every injured person brought for treatment should be given medical aid immediately to preserve life and thereafter the procedural criminal law should be allowed to operate in order to avoid negligent death. In the event of breach of this direction, apart from any action that may be taken for negligence, appropriate compensation should be given.

The petition appended a news report in which a person took an injured scooterist to the nearest hospital, only to be told that the victim should be taken to another hospital 20 km away, as that was the one authorised to handle medico-legal case. While the scooterist was being taken there, he died.

The Supreme Court issued notices to the Union Health Secretary, the Medical Council of India and the Indian Medical Association. There were no two opinions on the importance of giving urgent medical care to the accident victims. Several committees and conferences of these bodies had already discussed and took decisions on this question. The Code of Ethics drawn up by the Medical Council has stressed the duty of the doctor to care for a person seeking his help. A committee under the chairmanship of the Director-General of Health Services had laid down that whenever any medico-legal case comes to the hospital, the medical officer on duty should inform the duty constable the name, age and sex of the patient and the place and time of occurrence of the incident, and should start treatment ... full medical report should be prepared and given to the police as soon as examination and treatment of the patient is over. The treatment would not wait for the arrival of the police or completing legal formalities.

Decision: The court emphasised the duty of doctors in view of Article 21 of the Constitution guaranteeing life and liberty. No law or state action can intervene to avoid or delay this paramount obligation. "The obligation being total, absolute and paramount, laws of procedure which would interfere with the discharge of this obligation cannot be sustained and must, therefore, give way."

Every doctor must be reminded of his obligation and assured that he does not contravene law by proceeding to treat an injured person brought to him. "We must make it clear that zonal regulations and classifications cannot also operate as fetters in the process of discharge of the obligation and irrespective of the fact whether under instructions or rules the victim has to be sent elsewhere or how the police shall be contacted, the guideline indicated that the 1985 decision of the committee is to become operative."

The court, to give publicity to this judgement, directed the TV and radio to broadcast the decision. The court also asked the registry to send copies of the judgement to all high courts which will in turn forward it to district judges. They shall give due publicity to the judgement in their respective districts so that citizens and doctors are aware of their obligations.

There were two judges who heard the case. The ruling summarised so far was written by Justice R.N. Misra. The other judge, Justice G.L. Oza, while agreeing with his brother-judge, added another important point. Many doctors hesitate to take up injury cases fearing harassment by the police, lawyers and the courts for evidence. The judgement said that this apprehension, even if they have some foundation, should not prevent them from performing their duty. The court asked the police, the lawyers and judges and everyone concerned not to harass doctors for interrogation, cross-examination and formalities. Even when they have to be called, care should be taken to see that they are not made to wait and waste time unnecessarily.

68

V. Krishnakumar vs State of Tamil Nadu AIR 2015 SC 2836 = 2015 (9) SCC 388

For Medical Negligence, Compensation is payable to the consumer.

Facts: Supreme Court agreed with the findings of the NCDRC that the respondents were negligent in their duty and were deficient in their services in not screening the child between 2 to 4 weeks after birth when it is mandatory to do so and especially since the child was under their care. Thus, the negligence began under the supervision of the Hospital i.e. Respondent No.2. The Respondent Nos. 3 and 4, who checked the baby at his private clinic and at the appellant's home, respectively, were also negligent in not advising screening for ROP. It is pertinent to note that Respondent Nos. 3 and 4 carried on their own private practice while being in the employment of Respondent No. 2, which was a violation of their terms of service.

Decision: The question that falls for consideration is the compensation which the respondents are liable to pay for their negligence and deficiency in service. The child called Sharanya has been rendered blind for life. The darkness in her life can never be really compensated for in money terms. Blindness can have terrible consequences. Though, Sharanya may have parents now, there is no doubt that she will not have that protection and care forever. The family belongs to the middle class and it is necessary for the father to attend to his work. Undoubtedly, the mother would not be able to take Sharanya out everywhere and is bound to leave the child alone for reasonable spells of time. During this time, it is obvious that she would require help and maybe later on in life she would have to totally rely on such help. It is therefore difficult to imagine unhindered marriage prospects or even a regular career which she may have otherwise pursued with ease. She may also face great difficulties in getting education. The parents have already incurred heavy expenditure on the treatment of Sharanya to no avail. It is, thus, obvious that there should be adequate compensation for the expenses already incurred, the pain and suffering, lost wages and the future care that would be necessary while accounting for inflationary trends.

There is no doubt that in the future Sharanya would require further medical attention and would have to incur costs on medicines and possible surgery. It can be reasonably said that the blindness has put Sharanya at a great disadvantage in her pursuit for making a good living to care for herself.

At the outset, it may be noted that in such cases, this court has ruled out the computation of compensation according to the multiplier method.

The court rightly warned against the straightjacket approach of using the multiplier method for calculating damages in medical negligence cases.

Quantification of Compensation: The principle of awarding compensation that can be safely relied on is restitutioin integrum. This principle has been recognized and relied on in Balram Prasad's case (supra), in the following passage from the latter: "170. Indisputably, grant of compensation involving an accident is within the realm of law of torts. It is based on the principle of restitutio in integrum. The said principle provides that a person entitled to damages should, as nearly as possible, get that sum of money which would put him in the same position as he would have been if he had not sustained the wrong. (See Livingstone vs. Rawyards Coal Co.)." An application of this principle is that the aggrieved person should get that sum of money, which would put him in the same position if he had not sustained the wrong. It must necessarily result in compensating the aggrieved person for the financial loss suffered due to the event, the pain and suffering undergone and the liability that he/she would have to incur due to the disability caused by the event.

In the circumstances, we consider it appropriate to apportion the liability of ₹1,38,00,000/- among the respondents, as follows: ₹1,30,00,000/- shall be paid by Respondent Nos. 1 and 2 jointly and severally i.e. The State of Tamil Nadu and the Director, Government Hospital for Women & Children, Egmore, Chennai, and ₹8,00,000/- shall be paid by Respondent Nos. 3 and 4 equally i.e. ₹4,00,000/- by Dr. S. Gopaul, Neo- pediatrician, Government Hospital for Women & Children, Egmore, Chennai and ₹4,00,000/- by respondent No. 4 i.e. Dr. Duraisamy, Neo Natology Unit, Government Hospital for Women & Children, Egmore, Chennai.

69

State, Rep by Inspector of Police, Central Crime Branch vs R. Vasanthi Stanley

AIR 2015 SC 3691 = 2016 (1) SCC 376

Criminal Proceeding cannot be Quashed on the Ground of Gender - or on the Ground of Delay in trial or Settlement in cases of economic offences which are offences against the society.

Facts: The seminal issues that emanate for consideration, unequivocally on the bedrock of fiscal sanctity and decidedly on the plinth of prevalent mindset of borrowers from public financial institutions including banks, are whether a borrower or borrowers after availing finance by creating mortgage on the base of certain documents which, as alleged, are forged, and ingeniously adopt the same modus operandi to avail the benefit from number of banks, who in due course facing the problem set the criminal law in motion by lodging different FIRs and in the ultimate eventuate in an adroit manner enter into settlements and pay the amount and thereafter, knock at the doors of the High Court seeking exercise of inherent jurisdiction under Section 482 of the Code of Criminal Procedure (CrPC) or the extraordinary jurisdiction under Article 226 of the Constitution for quashment of the criminal proceedings; and should the High Court on the foundation that the continuance of the criminal proceedings would be a Sisyphean endeavour after the settlement has taken place to quash the same; and further whether a former Assistant Commissioner of Commercial Taxes can be allowed to advance a plea, obviously a remarkable one, that she had signed the documents either as a guarantor or as a co-applicant, showing deference to her late husband's desire; and, therefore, this Court, in exercise of power under Article 136 of the Constitution, should not unsettle the common order by which the High Court has quashed criminal proceedings. Additionally, it has also become obligatory to decisively lay down whether continuance of such proceedings would be an unnecessary load on the criminal justice dispensation system and hence, there is neither any warrant nor justification for interference with the order of the High Court.

Decision: It was held that economic offences are crimes against society and such offence is gender neutral. A grave criminal offence or serious economic offence or for that matter the offence that has the potentiality to create a dent in trial or the principle that when the matter has been settled, it should be quashed to avoid the load on the system. It was held that can never be an acceptable principle or parameter, for that will amount to destroying the stem cells of law and order in many a realm and further strengthen the marrows of the unscrupulous litigations.

70

A.K. Kraipak vs Union of India AIR 1970 SC 150

This was the first case in which Apex Court held that even purely administrative action is subject to judicial review.

Facts: Here the petitioner was a candidate for the selection of some post in Indian Forest Service. A special selection Board was constituted under Regulation 3 of Indian Forest Service (Initial Recruitinent) Regulation (1966) framed under Rule 3 of Indian Forest Service (Recruitment) Rules, 1966. One member of the Board was himself a candidate for selection. Though he did not take part in the deliberations of Board at the time of his own selection, he had taken part throughout while making selections of other candidates including his rival candidates. The petitioner contended that selection list prepared by such Board under Regulation 5 is vitiated and final recommendation made by Union Public Service Commission on its basis must also be vitiated, as there was reasonable likelihood of bias. The court upheld the contention of the petitioner and made the following historic observations.

Ruling: "Till very recently it was the opinion of the courts that unless the authority concerned was required by the law under which it functioned to act judicially there was no room for the application of the rules of natural justice. The validity of that limitation is now questioned. If the purpose of the rules of natural justice is to prevent miscarriage of justice there is no reason why those rules should he made in applicable to administrative enquiries. Arriving at a just decision is the aim of both quasi-judicial enquiries as wel' as adminis trative enquiries. An unjust decision in an administrative enquiry may have more far-reaching effect than a decision in quasi-judicial enquiry."

The court held the dividing line between an administrative power and a quasi judicial power is quite thin and is being gradually obliterated for determining whether a power is an administrative power or a quasi judicial power one has to look to the nature of the power conferred, the person or persons on whom it is conferred, the framework of the law conferring that power, the consequences ensuing from the exercise of that power and the manner in which that power is expected to be exercised. In a welfare state like India which is regulated and controlled by the rule of law, it is inevitable that the jurisdiction of the administrative bodies is increasing at a rapid rate. The concept of rule of law would lose its vitality if the instrumentalities of the state are not charged with the duty of discharging their functions in a fair and just manner. The requirement of acting judicially in essence is nothing but a requirement to act justly and fairly and not arbitrarily or capriciously. The procedures which are considered inherent in the exercise of a judicial power are merely those which facilitate if not ensure a just and fair decision. In recent years the concept of quasi-judicial power has been undergoing a radical change. What was considered as an administrative power some years backs is now being considered as a quasi-judicial power.

71

TSR Subramanian vs Union of India,(2013) 15 SCC 732

Subordinate officer is not bound to carry out the illegal orders of the superior officer.

Facts: The petitioners were retired top civil servants from the IAS and the IPS. They sought mandatory court injunctions to support the independence of the various Indian civil services and their freedom from political interference, by requiring the Indian federal and state governments to implement the recommendations made by several commissions of review : that oral instructions given by politicians to civil servants must be recorded in writing, that senior civil service appointments should be made for a fixed term, and that civil services boards should be established to advise on postings. In addition, politicians in state government were seen to have been transferring civil servants repeatedly.

Decision by the Supreme Court:

- Officers of the IAS, other All India Services and other civil servants were not bound to follow oral directives, as they "undermine credibility."
- Establishment of a Civil Services Board (CSB), headed by the Cabinet Secretary at the national level and chief secretaries at the state level, to recommend transfers and postings of All India Services officers. However, the Appointments Committee of the Cabinet will be the final authority for transfer of officers under the Central Staffing Scheme.
- It also directed the respective governments to set out terms of tenure for different types of civil servants within three months.
- Group 'B' officers would be transferred by heads of departments.
- No interference of ministers, other than the chief minister, in transfers or postings of civil servants at the state level.

Comments: It some of these directives of the Supreme Court are implemented, it will help to cleanse the system considerably.

72

Vineet Narain vs Union of India, (1998) 1 SCC 226

No sanction is required by CBI to prosecute high officials and ministers.

Facts: This case concerns the historic Hawala scandal in India, which uncovered possible bribery payments to several high-ranking Indian politicians and bureaucrats from a funding source linked to suspected terrorists. Following news coverage of the scandal, members of the public were dismayed by the failure of the Central Bureau of Investigation (CBI) to initiate investigations of the officials with the apparent intent to protect certain implicated individuals who were extremely influential in government and politics. This litigation was the result of public interest petitions filed on these matters with the Court pursuant to Article 32 of the Indian Constitution

Decision:

- All thc cases unfortunately collapsed at the stage of prosecution in court.
- The Court agreed that the CBI had failed in its responsibility to investigate allegations of public corruption. It laid down guidelines to ensure independence and autonomy of the CBI and ordered that the CBI be placed under the supervision of the Central Vigilance Commission (CVC), an independent governmental agency intended to be free from executive control or interference. This directive removed the CBI from the supervision of the Central Government thought to be partly responsible for the inertia that contributed to the CBI's previous lack of urgency with respect to the investigation of high-ranking officials. The CVC is now responsible for ensuring that allegations of corruption against public officials were thoroughly investigated

regardless of the identity of the accused and without interference from the Government.

- The Court in this case had struck down the validity of a directive issued by the Ministries and Departments in the Central Government that required the CBI to seek approval of the Central Government before pursuing investigation against bureaucrats of the level of Joint Secretary and above on grounds that it violated the independence of the investigative process.

Comments: These observations of the Supreme Court should be implemented keeping in view that the decision-making at the crucial level of Joint Secetory, GOI and above is not adversely affected. At the same time, according sanction for prosecution in bribery cases should not be delayed by senior bureaucrats and politicians alike.

73

Prakash Singh and Ors. vs Union of India and Ors.
(2006) 85 SCC 1
Implement police reforms.

Facts: In 1996, Mr Prakash Singh, a retired police officer, petitioned the Supreme Court under Article 32, urging for the issue of directions to the Government of India to frame a new Police Act on the lines of the model Act drafted by the Commission in order to ensure that the police is made accountable essentially and primarily to law of the land and the people. The petitioners attributed the abuse of power and inefficient functioning of the police to archaic structure and organisation outlined in the Police Act, 1861.

Decision: The Supreme Court issued various directions to the centre and states, including:

- Constitute a State Security Commission in every state that will lay down policy for police functioning, evaluate police performance, and ensure that state governments do not exercise unwarranted influence on the police.
- Constitute Police Complaints Authorities at the state and district levels to inquire into allegations of serious misconduct and abuse of power by police personnel.
- Provide a minimum tenure of at least two years for the DGP and other key police officers within the state forces.
- Ensure that the DGP of state police is appointed from amongst three senior-most officers who have been empanelled for the promotion by the Union Public Service Commission on the basis of length of service, good record and experience.
- Constitute a National Security Commission to shortlist the candidates for appointment as Chiefs of the central armed police forces.

- Separation of Investigation: The investigating police shall be separated from the law-and-order police to ensure speedier investigation, better expertise and improved rapport with the people. It must, however, be ensured that there is full coordination between the two wings. The separation, to start with, may be affected in towns/ urban areas which have a population of ten lakhs or more, and gradually extended to smaller towns/urban areas also. Police Establishment Board: There shall be a Police Establishment Board in each State which shall decide all transfers, postings, promotions and other service-related matters of officers of and below the rank of Deputy Superintendent of Police. The Establishment Board shall be a departmental body comprising the Director General of Police and four other senior officers of the Department. The State Government may interfere with decision of the Board in exceptional cases only after recording its reasons for doing so. The Board shall also be authorized to make appropriate recommendations to the State Government regarding the posting and transfers of officers of and above the rank of Superintendent of Police, and the Government is expected to give due weight to these recommendations and shall normally accept it. It shall also function as a forum of appeal for disposing of representations from officers of the rank of Superintendent of Police and above regarding their promotion/transfer/disciplinary proceedings or their being subjected to illegal or irregular orders and generally reviewing the functioning of the police in the State.

Comments: Implementation of police reforms is a need of the hour. The police reforms may be implemented in phases but promptly.

74

In Re case in Writ Petition (Civil) No. 1099 of 2019 and Others

Regarding Abrogation of Article 370 of the Constitution relating to Jammu & Kashmir

Decision of the Supreme Court relating to abrogation of Article 370 is an epoch making judgment and has an historical impact like the Ayodhya Judgment to install Ramlala.

Facts: On 26th October, 1947, the then Maharaja of Jammu and Kashmir Maharaj Hari Singh through an Instrument of Accession accepted the accession of Jammu and Kashmir and merged with the Union of India retaining certain autonomy. Accordingly, Indian Government was entrusted with defence, foreign affairs and communication. However, the Preamble of the Constitution of Jammu and Kashmir recognized Jammu and Kashmir as integral part of the Union of India.

Later on by the Constitution Amendments in 1950,1958 and in 1955,1956 and 1965, Jammu and Kashmir were sought to make J&K similar to other States of India. People in other parts of India did not like the special status to J&K as the state used its separate flag and enjoyed lot of autonomy specially in view of separatist tendencies in the state and more in view of terrorist activities sponsored from across the international border by Pakistan and its terrorist outfits.

In a sudden move on 5th August, 2019, the President of India issued an order that firstly, all the provisions of the Constitution of India shall apply in relation to the state of Jammu and Kashmir and secondly, the Legislative Assembly of the state shall be treated as the Constituent Assembly of India. On 6th August, 2019, the President, on the recommendation of Parliament, made a declaration that from 6th August, 2019, all clauses of Article 370 shall cease to be operative except the following:

"**370.** All provisions of the Constitution, as amended from time to time, without any modifications or exceptions, shall apply to the State of Jammu and Kashmir notwithstanding anything contrary contained in Article 152 or Article 308 or any other Article of the Constitution or any other provision of the Constitution of Jammu and Kashmir or any law, document, judgement, ordinance, order by law, rule, regulation, notification, custom or usage having the force of law in the territory of India, or any other instrument, treaty or agreement as envisaged under Article 363 or otherwise."

Later, State of Jammu and Kashmir was reorganized into two union territories i.e. Union Territory of Jammu and Kashmir with a Legislative Assembly under Article 239A and Union Territory of Ladakh.

The above amendments of the Constitution by Presidential order with the concurrence of Parliament, were challenged before the Apex Court through various writ petitions.

Decision: After hearing all concerned parties, the five judges Bench of the Supreme Court headed by the Chief Justice of India Dr. D.Y. Chandrachud, upheld the validity of the abrogation of Article 370 and delivered the following judgment unanimously:

a. The State of Jammu and Kashmir does not retain any element of sovereignty after the execution of the Instrument of Accession and issuance of the Proclamation dated 26 November 1949 by which the Constitution of India was adopted. The State of Jammu and Kashmir does not have 'internal sovereignty' which is distinguishable from the powers and privileges enjoyed by other states in the country. Article 370 was a feature of asymmetric federalism and not sovereignty;
b. The petitioners did not challenge the issuance of the Proclamation under Section 92 of the Jammu and Kashmir Constitution and Article 356 of the Indian Constitution until

the special status of Jammu and Kashmir was abrogated. The challenge to the Proclamations does not merit adjudication because the principal challenge is to the actions which were taken after the Proclamation was issued;

c. The exercise of power by the President after the Proclamation under Article 356 is issued in subject to judicial review. The exercise of power by the President must have a reasonable nexus with the object of the Proclamation. The person challenging the exercise of power must prima facie establish that it is a mala fide or extraneous exercise of power. Once a prima facie case is made, the onus shifts to the Union to justify the exercise of such power;

d. The power of Parliament under Article 356(1)(b) to exercise the powers of the Legislature of the State cannot be restricted to law-making power thereby excluding non-law making power of the Legislature of the State. Such an interpretation would amount to reading in a limitation into the provision contrary to the text of the Article;

e. It can be garnered from the historical context for the inclusion of Article 370 and the placement of Article 370 in Part xxi of the Constitution that it is a temporary provision;

f. The power under Article 370(3) did not cease to exist upon the dissolution of the Constituent Assembly of Jammu and Kashmir. When the Constituent Assembly was dissolved, only the transitional power recognized in the proviso to Article 370(3) which empowered the Constituent Assembly to make its recommendations ceased to exist. It did not affect the power held by the President under Article 370(3);

g. Article 370 cannot be amended by exercise of power under Article 370(1)(d). Recourse must have been taken to the procedure contemplated by Article 370(3) if Article 370 is to cease to operate or is to be amended or modified in its application to the State of Jammu and Kashmir. Paragraph 2 of CO 272 by which Article was amended through Article 367 is ultra vires Article 370(1)(d) because it modifies Article 370, in effect, without following the procedure prescribed to modify Article 370. An interpretation clause cannot be used to bypass the procedure laid down for amendment;

h. The exercise of power by the President under Article370(1)(d) to issue CO 272 is not mala fide. The President in exercise of power under Article 370(3) can unilaterally issue a notification that Article 370 ceases to exist. The President did not have to secure the concurrence of the Government of the State or Union Government acting on behalf of the State Government under the second proviso to Article 370(1)(d) while applying all the provisions of the Constitution to Jammu and Kashmir because such an exercise of power has the same effect as an exercise of power under Article 370(3) for which the concurrence or collaboration with the State Government was not required;

i. Paragraph 2 of CO 272 issued by the President in exercise of power under Article 370(1)(d) applying all the provisions of the Constitution of India to the State of Jammu and Kashmir is valid. Such an exercise of power is not mala fide merely because all the provisions were applied together without following a piece-meal approach;

j. The President had the power to issue a notification declaring that Article 370(3) ceases to operate without the recommendation of the Constituent Assembly. The continuous exercise of power under Article 370(1) by the President indicates that the gradual process of constitutional integration was ongoing. The declaration issued by the President under Article 370(3) is a culmination of the process of integration and as such is a valid exercise of power. Thus, CO 273 is valid;

k. The Constitution of India is a complete code for constitutional governance. Following the application of the Constitution of India in its entirety to the State of Jammu and Kashmir by CO 273, the Constitution of the State of Jammu and Kashmir is inoperative and is declared to have become redundant;

l. The views of the Legislature of the State under the first proviso of Article are recommendatory. Thus, Parliament's exercise of power under the first proviso of Article 3, under the Proclamation was valid and not mala fide.

m. The Solicitor General stated that the statehood of Jammu and Kashmir will be restored (except for the carving out of the Union Territory of Ladakh). In view of the statement we do not find it necessary to determine whether the reorganization of the State of Jammu and Kashmir into two Union Territories of Ladakh and Jammu and Kashmir is permissible under Article 3. However, we uphold the validity of the decision to carve out the Union Territory of Ladakh in view of Article 3(a) read with explanation which permits forming a Union Territory by separation of a territory from any State; and

n. We direct that steps shall be taken by the Election Commission of India to conduct elections for the Legislative Assembly of Jammu and Kashmir constituted under Section 14 of the Reorganisation Act by 30 September 2024. Restoration of statehood shall take place at the earliest and as soon as possible.

Thus, the writ petition and special leave petitions were disposed off by the Supreme Court in the above terms.

Comments: The decision of the Supreme Court has once again established the sovereignty and integrity of India throughout the territory of India. The separatist tendencies in Jammu and Kashmir have been checkmated and terrorism has been checked. The public, in general has got a sigh of relief as perpetration of violence in Jammu and Kashmir had caused public uproar. However, it is not understood why this simple constitutional interpretation could not come earlier. It speaks poorly of our system which should have taken such a decision even without a Supreme Court ruling. However, the Supreme Court's decision should now be implemented to the letter and spirit and Jammu and Kashmir State should be given full statehood after union territory of Ladakh is carved out of it with certain special provisions like the North Eastern States in the Sixth Schedule of the Constitution of India.

75

Union Carbide Corporation & Others vs Union of India & Others AIR 1992 SC 248 = 1991 (4) SCC 584

Bhopal Gas Leak Disaster Case & Bhopal Gas Peedit Mamla Udyog Sanghatan vs Union of India 1989 AIR SC 1069

Facts: Government of India assured to withdraw the suit filed by it in the Dist. Court of Bhopal and also gave a word that it may not pursue any criminal action against Union Carbide. Thereafter some interested third parties filed a review petition claiming that the settlement arrived at being without jurisdiction, shall be set aside. It may be noted here that before the settlement is recorded, all of the cases pending at the Dist. Court of Bhopal are withdrawn.

The main questions raised in this review petition are that the Supreme Court was not competent to order in exercise of its powers under Sections 136 and 142 in a manner detrimental to the interest of parties and that the agreement recorded by the Supreme Court is unfair and since the agreement is intended stifling of prosecution. It is opposed to public policy. While rejecting all the contentions in an apologetic manner, the Court issued directions as to the manner in which the relief measures to be undertaken must be disposed of expeditiously setting up a fair procedure therefore.

Decision: There were no legal questions involved in the case. Therefore, there are no long judgements, but only a series of small orders. The petitioners complained about inadequacies in the distribution of interim relief including milk, bread, sugar and edible oils. The court, often a Constitution bench itself, passed necessary orders on them. By this process, the Supreme Court has maintained a continuous watch on the relief measures for Bhopal victims. This process went on for years, new judges continuing the monitoring of the relief measures. The petitioners and the court have put some accountability on the authorities, in the absence of which the relief measures would have been even more tardy.

Comment: This is one case in which the Supreme Court decision is still not very effective as all Bhopal Gas Vectims have still not got justice by way of treatment and their resettlement. Everyone is failing to tackle the greatest enemy 'delay'.

76

K.N. Govindacharya vs Union of India and Ors.

W.P. (C) 3672/2012 dated 23/08/2013

Social media companies should place grievance officers and their servers in India.

Facts: In this Public Interest Litigation filed before the High Court of Delhi, the petitioner challenged the usage of social media by minors, government officers and agencies and further sought appointment of a Grievance Officer as per Information Technology (Intermediary Guidelines), Rules, 2011. The petitioner also prayed for bringing social media companies such as Facebook and Orkut under the tax ambit for their monetization of data of Indian users. The petitioner contended that the presence of minors on such social media platforms is violative of Indian Contract Act, 1872 and the usage of such platforms by Government is breach of Public Records Act, 1933.

Decision: In its order dated 23.08.2013, the Court directed Facebook and Orkut for removal of accounts of children below 13 years of age in accordance with the Rule 3(1)-3(4) of Information Technology (Intermediary Guidelines), Rules, 2011. In accordance with the Rule 3(11) of the afore-mentioned Rules, the Court directed that "intermediaries, including the social networking sites such as Facebook and Orkut, should immediately publish the names of the respective Grievance Officers on their websites along with contact numbers as well as the mechanism by which any user or any victim who suffers as a result of access or usage of computer resource by any person in violation of rule 3. The same be complied with, if not already done, within two weeks." The Court also directed the Union to frame policy qua usage of social media by the Government. The said policy was finalized and submitted before the Court. It also stated that an office memorandum was issued advising all the government employees to follow a particular protocol and that for any official work involving transmission of public records, they must use an e-mail identity connected to a server located in India and can connect with National Informatics Centre (NIC).

Comments: Inspite of above direction of the court, grievance officers are yet to be in place in India by various social media, less to place their servers and to pay taxes in India.

77

Visakha & Others, Petitioners vs State of Rajasthan & Others, Respondents

AIR 1997 SC 3011 = 1997 (6) SCC 241

Guidelines for prevention of sexual harassment of women at work places

Facts: An application coming under the category public interest litigation is filed in the Supreme Court requesting the Court to issue some guidelines which can prevent sexual harassment of women in work places, a phenomena against which there has been a public outcry. The Court after referring to Arts. 15, 42, 51, 51(A) and 253 accepted the application and issued the following directions.

Ruling: The Court held: "Taking note of the fact that the present civil and criminal laws in India do not adequately provide for specific protection of women from sexual harassment in work places and that enactment of such legislation will take considerable time; it is necessary and expedient for the employers in work places as well as other responsible persons or institutions to observe certain guidelines to ensure the prevention of sexual harassment of women.

1. *Duty of the Employer or other responsible persons in work places and other institutions:* It shall be the duty of the employer or other responsible persons in work places or other institutions to prevent or deter the commission of acts of sexual harassment and to provide the procedures for the resolution, settlement or prosecution of acts of sexual harassment by taking all steps required.
2. *Definition:* For this purpose, sexual harassment includes such unwelcome sexually determined behaviour (whether directly or by implication) as:
   (a) physical contact and advances;
   (b) a demand or request for sexual favours;
   (c) sexually coloured remarks;

(d) showing pornography;

(e) any other unwelcome physical, verbal or non-verbal conduct of sexual nature.

Where any of these acts is committed in circumstances whereunder the victim of such conduct has a reasonable apprehension that in relation to the victim's emplooyment or work whether she is drawing salary, or honorarium or voluntary, whether in Government, public or private enterprise such conduct can be humiliating and may constitute a health and safety prolem. It is discriminatory for instance when the woman has reasonable grounds to believe that her objection would disadvantage her in connection with her employment or work including recruiting or promotion or when it creates a hostile work environment. Adverse consequences might be visited if the victim does not consent to the conduct in question or raises any objection thereto.

3. *Preventive Steps:* All employers or persons in charge of work place whether in the public or private sector should take appropriate steps to prevent sexual harassment. Without prejudice to the generality of this obligation they should take the following steps:

(a) Express prohibition of sexual harassment as defined above at the work place should be notified, published and circulated in appropriate ways.

(b) The Rules/Regulations of Government and Public Sector bodies relating to conduct and discipline should include rules/regulations prohibiting sexual harassment and provide for appropriate penalties in such rules against the offender.

(c) As regards private employers steps should be taken to include the aforesaid prohibitions in the standing orders under the Industrial Employment (Standing Orders) Act, 1946.

(d) Appropriate work conditions should be provided in respect of work, leisure, health and hygiene to further ensure that there is no hostile environment towards women at work places and no employee woman should have reasonable grounds to believe that she is disadvantage din connection with her employment.

4. *Criminal Proceedings:* Where such conduct amounts to a specific offence under the Indian Penal Code or under any other law, the employer shall initiate appropriate action in accordance with law by making a complaint with the appropriate authority.

   In particular, it should ensure that victims, or witnesses are not victimized or discriminated against while dealing with complaints of sexual harassment. The victims of sexual harassment should have the option to seek transfer of the perpetrator or their own transfer.

5. *Disciplinary action:* Where such conduct amounts to misconduct in employment as defined by the relevant service rules, appropriate disciplinary action should be initiated by the employer in accordance with those rules.

6. *Complaint Mechanism:* Whether or not such conduct constitutes an offence under law or a breach of the service rules, an appropriate complaint mechanism should be created in the employer's organization for redress of the complaint made by the victim. Such complaint mechanism should ensure time bound treatment of complaints.

7. *Complaints Committee:* The complaint mechanism, referred to in (6) above, should be adequate to provide, where necessary, a Complaints Committee, a special counsellor or other support service, including the maintenance of confidentiality.

   The Complaints Committee should be headed by a woman and not less than half of its member should be women. Further, to prevent the possibility of any undue pressure or influence from senior levels, such Complaints Committee should involve a third party, either NGO or other body who is familiar with the issue of sexual harassment.

   The Complaints Committee must make an annual report to the Government department concerned of the complaints and action taken by them.

   The employers and person in charge will also report on the compliance with the aforesaid guidelines including on the reports of the Complaints Committee to the Government department.

8. *Workers' Initiative:* Employees should be allowed to raise issues of sexual harassment at workers' meeting and in other appropriate forum and it should be affirmatively discussed in Employer-Employee Meetings.
9. *Awareness:* Awareness of the rights of female employees in this regard should be created in particular by prominently notifying the guidelines (and appropriate legislation when enacted on the subject) in a suitable manner.
10. *Third Party Harassment:* Where sexual harassment occurs as a result of an act or omission by any third party or outsider, the employer and person in charge will take all steps necessary and reasonable to assist the affected person in terms of support and prventive action.
11. The Central/State Governments are requested to consider adopting suitable measures including legislation to ensure that the guidelines laid down by this order are also observed by the employers in Private Sector.
12. These guidelines will not prejudice any rights available under the Protection of Human Rights Act, 1993.

Accordingly, we direct that the above guidelines and norms would be strictly observed in all work places for the preservation and enforcement of the right to gender equality of the working women. These directions would be binding and enforceable in law until suitable legislation is enacted to occupy the field. These Writ Petitions are disposed of, accordingly."

Comment: The Govt. of India or any State Government have not passed any enactment on this subject. But they have issued only several executive instructions which apply to not only the Govt. offices but also to the private establisments. These guidelines are effective as good as any enactment made by Parliament which amounts to law making by the judiciary.

The Central Government however enacted an Act called Protection of Women from Domestic Violence Act, 2005.

78

Subrata Roy Sahara vs UOI and Others (2014) 8 SCC 470

Detention of Sahara Chief Subrata Roy in Jail for non-payment of public dues under Articles 129 and 142 of the Constitution of India

Facts: Sahara India moved the Supreme Court for contempt of court against SEBI seeking a ₹62,000 crore deposit with them which caused public outrage against Sahara. Thousands of innocent Depositors where waiting for their refund from the non-banking companies of Sahara India who felt deceived and defrauded. SEBI canceled the license of Sahara Mutual Fund business.

Decision: The Supreme Court in its order dated February 2017 directed that Sahara India had committed utter disregard of their direction to deposit principal and interest. Subrata Roy, Sahara Chief was arrested by U.P. Police for failure to appear before the Supreme Court in February 2014. In March, 2014, he was sent to Tihar Jail along with two other directors of Sahara India.

After a long detention, Subrata Roy was released on parole in May, 2016. However Sahara Credit Co-operation Socicty is allowed to make payment to creditors / investors by Delhi High Court.

Subsequently Sahara deposited ₹22,500 crores with the SEBI in Sahara Refund Account against the principal amount of ₹24,029.73 crore.

SEBI has repaid only ₹107 crores to 19,532 claims as per report. SEBI has not conducted further exercise of verification of 3.03 crore investors. SEBI has incurred about ₹100 crore to invite the claimants to make their outstanding payments.

Comments: The case is first of its kind as many Chit Funds Companies deceive the innocent depositors. After this detention of Sahara Chief in the court's custody and also of many real-estate chiefs, message has gone to the commercial heads that they can not afford to play with the financial investors of public in the garb of pending court cases or otherwise. Similarly, the directors of companies cann't hide behind curtain of the company as legal entity. They are also now personally liable after new law and court's ruling.

Lily Thomas vs Union of India, (2000) 6 SCC 224

The balance between Directive Principles and Fundamental Rights is a basic structure of the Constitution.

Facts:

Sushmita Ghosh filed a petition before the apex court stating that she was married to Mr. M C Ghosh as per Hindu rituals since the year 1984. However, in the year 1992, Mr. Ghosh asked Ms. Ghosh for divorce by mutual consent while stating that he had converted to Islam so that he can marry for the second time to Ms. Vinita Gupta who was a divorcee with two kids. There is no provision for a second marriage or bigamy under the Hindu Marriage Act, 1959, so he also produced a certificate which confirmed that he had converted to Islam. It is amply clear from the above-stated facts that Mr. Ghosh only converted to Islam because he wanted to contract a second marriage and that he had actually no faith in his converted religion. The instant petition brought to the fore several important issues for the court to deal with and adjudicate on the issue of implementation of a Uniform Civil Code as envisaged by Article 44 of the Constitution. Another important question before the Court was whether a Hindu husband in order to contract a second marriage can convert to Islam; where such a marriage is permitted what was the validity of the first and the second marriage respectively. Also, when such a husband contracts such a second marriage, should he be prosecuted for Bigamy under Section 494 of the Indian Penal Code?

Judgement:

❖ The Court held that when a second marriage is contracted by a Hindu husband after conversion, he does not do so because of his conscience and that such a conversion is manifestly fraudulent and is feigned in order to achieve an ulterior motive (which is to contract a second marriage without getting prosecuted for the same).

- Therefore, it was laid down that such a marriage was void and invalid due to the violation of Article 21.
- A marriage cannot be deemed to have been dissolved simply because a husband has converted to a different religion.
- A marriage contracted by converting to Islam while the first one is subsisting will invite penal action under different provisions of the Indian Penal Code.
- In India, there are no marriage-related laws since marriage takes place according to one's personal law.
- Therefore, such things could not be codified and applying the uniform civil code to such an issue would not do justice to one's own personal belief.
- But what could be penalized are the wrong acts done in the pretext of such personal law, which is what the SC has done in this case by making it illegal to marry another person by converting to Islam while already in marriage with the first wife.

Comment: One can not be allowed to bypass a law fraudulently.

80

IR Coelho vs State of Tamil Nadu, AIR 2007 SC 861

Insertion of an Act in the Ninth Schedule does not make it immune from the judicial review.

Facts:

The Gudalur Janmann Estates (Abolition and Conversion into Ryotwari), Act, 1969, in so far as it vested forest lands in the Janman estates in the State of Tamil Nadu, was struck down by the Court in Balmadies Plantations Ltd and Anr. vs. State of Tamil Nadu because this was not found to be a measure of agrarian reform protected by Article 31-A of the Constitution. Section 2(c) of the West Bengal Land Holding Revenue Act, 1979 was struck down by the Calcutta High Court as being arbitrary and, therefore, unconstitutional and the special leave petition filed against the judgment by the State of West Bengal was dismissed. Consequently, by the Constitution (Thirty-Fourth 34th Amendment) Act, and the Constitution (Sixty – Sixth 66th Amendment) Act, the Janman Act and the West Bengal Land Holding Revenue, Act. 1979, in its entirety was inserted in the Ninth Schedule. These insertions were the subject matter of challenge.

Judgement:

- In this case, a nine-member bench of Supreme Court held that Ninth schedule items are not immune to judicial review as it is part of the Constitution.
- Further, nothing in the Ninth schedule can abrogate fundamental rights as they form basic features of the Constitution.
- The objective behind Article 31B of the Constitution is to remove difficulties and not to wipe out judicial review per se.
- Therefore every amendment to the Constitution including amendment to the Ninth schedule has to be in accordance with the basic structure doctrine.

Comment: Apex Court should appreciate the wisdom of the legislature as they are closer to ground realities.

81

Government of NCT of Delhi vs Union of India, (2018) 8 SCC 501

Lieutenant Governor cannot function independently on matters not exclusively entrusted to him.

Facts:

- In April 2015, Najeeb Jung who was Lieutenant Governor of Delhi at that time made a statement that he is not required to send information regarding Police, Land & Public Order to Chief Minister's office under any law. Home Ministry also supported the LG stating that these three entries fall exclusively in the ambit of LG and therefore are not covered by aid & advice principle. There were many instances which led to the filing of the appeal into Supreme Court.
- Home Ministry stated that Delhi's state ACB does not have the power to investigate upon Central Government employees on aforementioned matters.
- The LG stayed the decision of the Delhi government to increase circle rates on agriculture land.
- Government of Delhi constituted a commission to investigate into CNG fitness scam allegation matter and that was overturned by Home Ministry by saying that the government does not have the power to set up a commission. Therefore, declared it to be void.
- Delhi government again constituted a commission to investigate into a scam of Delhi & District Cricket Association. It was declared invalid by the Home Ministry by stating the same reason.

- All these continuous events led to a contradiction between the LG & the CM.

Judgement:

- The Supreme Court ruled that according to the Article 239AA of the Indian Constitution, although the government had to keep him or her informed of its decisions, Delhi's lieutenant governor had no independent decision-making powers and had to follow the aid and advice of the Chief-minister-led Council of Ministers of the Government of Delhi on matters the Delhi Legislative Assembly could legislate on, viz., all items on the State List (items on which only state legislatures can legislate) and the Concurrent List (items on which both the Parliament of India and the state legislatures can legislate) barring police, public order and land.
- The court added that on matters referred to him/her, the LG was bound to follow the orders of the President. Aid & advice principle is only applicable where the Legislature has the power to legislate and not on matters on which LG has exclusive power or exercises his discretion. His opinion focussed on a representative form of government should be the executive head. It was held that the LG's power to act independently violates the provision of representative government

Comment: In UTs with Legislative Assembly, L.G. should give due regard to aid and advice of the Chief Minister.

82

Vineeta Sharma vs Rakesh Sharma, Civil Appeal No. 32601 of 2018 Daughters would have equal coparcenary rights.

Facts:

❖ The Hindu Succession Act of 1956 recognized, under Section 6, the special right of male coparceners of a Hindu Coparcenary to inherit by birth over the coparcenary property and laid down rules for succession among the coparceners. This, however, was discriminatory in terms of gender and also negation of constitutional right of equality, in so far as the daughter of a coparcener was concerned.

❖ After the amendment issue was whether the rights of the daughter would be there if her father was not alive on the date on commencement of the amendment i.e. the 9th of September 2005. People had a lot of doubt regarding the nature of this provision if it was prospective in nature or retrospective or retroactive.

Judgement:

❖ Explaining obstructed and unobstructed heritage, the Hon'ble Supreme Court held that the unobstructed heritage takes place by birth, whereas the obstructed heritage takes place after the death of the owner. The Hon'ble Supreme Court further went on to hold that under Section 6, right is given by birth, making it an unobstructed heritage, and therefore coparcener father need be alive as on 09.09.2005 in order for the daughter to inherits rights over the coparcenary property.

❖ The Court also added that the concept of uncodified Hindu Law of unobstructed heritage has been given a concrete shape under the provisions of Section 6(1)(a) and 6(1)(b) and that the coparcenary right is by birth and therefore, it is not at all necessary that the father of the daughter be living as on the date of the amendment, since she had not been conferred with the rights of coparcener by obstructed heritage. As such, the Hon'ble Supreme Court did not consider decision in Phulavati case to be a good decision in so far as this aspect is concerned.

- As regards the applicability of the amended section 6 to be retrospective or prospective, the Hon'ble Supreme Court held that the amended Section 6 is retroactive in nature.

Comment: The ruling has improved social status of daughters. It has big impact on Hindu Joint Family system.

83

Swapnil Tripathi vs Supreme Court of India, 2018 (11) SCC 475 Live Streaming of exceptional cases in the Supreme Court is permissible.

Facts:

- Petitioners have sought a declaration that Supreme Court case proceedings of constitutional and national importance having an impact on the public at large or a large number of people should be live streamed in a manner that is easily accessible for public viewing. Further direction is sought to frame guidelines to enable the determination of exceptional cases that qualify for live streaming and to place those guidelines before the full court of this court.

Judgement:

- All cases brought before the courts, whether civil, criminal or others must be heard in open court. For a healthy, objective and fair administration of justice, what is needed is a public trial in open court. Trial held subject to the public scrutiny and gaze naturally acts as a check against judicial caprice or vagaries and serves as a powerful instrument for creating confidence of the public in the fairness, objectivity and impartiality of the administration of justice. Justice is found to be residing in a place where there is ample publicity. It acts as a guardian against improbity.
- Our legal system subscribes to the principle of open justice. Open justice is a long-established principle of common law systems. It rests on a high pedestal in a liberal democracy as a 'sound and a very sacred part of the Constitution of the country and the administration of justice.' It operates as a wholesome check upon judicial behaviour as well as upon the conduct of the contending parties and their witnesses.

- But if excessive publicity itself operates as an instrument of injustice, court may hold the trial behind closed doors and forbid publication of the report of its proceedings.
- The right to know and receive information is a facet of Article 19(1)(a) of the Constitution and for this reason the public is entitled to witness court proceedings involving issues having an impact on the public at large or a section of the public. State is obligated to spread awareness about the law and developments thereof including the evolution of the law which may happen in the process of adjudication of cases before this court.

Comment: Allowing streaming of Court proceedings of cases of Constitutional and national importance shows that the Supreme Court does what it expects others to do.

84

People's Union for Civil Liberties vs Union of India & Anr., (2013) 10 SCC 1

NOTA (None of the Above) may be provided in EVM.

Facts:

The present writ petition, under Article 32 of the Constitution of India, has been filed by the petitioners herein challenging the constitutional validity of Rules 41(2) & (3) and 49-O of the Conduct of Election Rules, 1961 (in short 'the Rules') to the extent that these provisions violate the secrecy of voting which is fundamental to the free and fair elections and is required to be maintained as per Section 128 of the Representation of the People Act, 1951 (in short 'the RP Act') and Rules 39 and 49-M of the Rules.

Judgement:

The Supreme Court of India judgement said, "*We direct the Election Commission to provide necessary provision in the ballot papers/EVMs and another button called "None of the Above" (NOTA) which may be provided in EVMs so that the voters, who come to the polling booth and decide not to vote for any of the candidates in the fray, are able to exercise their right not to vote while maintaining their right of secrecy.*" The Supreme Court also observed that it is essential that people of high moral and ethical values are chosen as people's representatives for proper governance of the country, and NOTA button can compel political parties to nominate a sound candidate.

Comment: It is one of the directions by the Supreme Court to cleanse the elections in India.

85

Vodafone International Holdings vs Union of India, (2012) 6 SCC 613

Bona fide expectations of corporates from the declared policy should be honoured by the Government.

Facts:

Vodafone International Holding (VIH) and Hutchison telecommunication international limited or HTIL are two non-resident companies. These companies entered into transaction by which HTIL transferred the share capital of its subsidiary company based in Cayman Island i.e. CGP international or CGP to VIH. VIH by virtue of this transaction acquired a controlling interest of 67 percent in Hutch is on Essar Limited or HEL that was an Indian Joint venture company (between Hutchinson and Essar) because CGP was holding the above 67 percent interest prior to the above deal. The Indian Revenue authorities issued a show cause notice to VIH as to why it should not be considered as "assessee in default" and thereby sought an explanation as to why the tax was not deducted on the sale consideration of this transaction. The Indian revenue authorities thereby through this sought to tax capital gain arising from sale of share capital of CGP on the ground that CGP had underlying Indian Assets. VIH filed a writ petition in the High Court challenging the jurisdiction of Indian revenue authorities. This writ petition was dismissed by the High Court and VIH appealed to the Supreme Court which sent the matter to Revenue authorities to decide whether the revenue had the jurisdiction over the matter. The revenue authorities decided that it had the jurisdiction over the matter and then matter went to High Court which was also decided in favour of Revenue and then finally Special Leave petition was filed in the Supreme Court.

Judgement:

The apex court pronounced a landmark judgment in Vodafone International Holding vs Union of India and cleared the uncertainty with respect to imposition of taxes. The apex court through this judgment recognized:

- The principles of tax planning.
- Business entities or individual may arrange the affairs of their business so as to reduce their tax liability in absence of any statutory stipulation prohibiting the same.
- The multinational companies often establish corporate structures and all these structures should be established for business and commercial purposes only.
- The corporate veil may be lifted in case facts and circumstances reveal that the transaction or corporate structure is sham and intended to evade taxes.
- The transactions should be looked holistic manner and not in a dissecting manner and the presence of corporate structures in tax neutral/investor friendly nations should not lead to the conclusion that these are meant to avoid taxes.

Comment: While inposing tax on multinational companies, future investment in the country should be kept in mind. However sham transaction on corporate structure intended to evade taxes should be duly brought to books.

Miscellaneous Cases in Brief

1. **Narmada Bachao Andolan Case:** This case on resettlement and rehabilitation was reported in Narmada Bachao Andolan vs. Union of India, AIR 2000 SC 3751
2. **Divorce of Muslim Woman:** Muslim women is entitled to maintenance under Section 125 Cr.P.C. from the date of divorce till she is remarried even after the Protection of a Divorced Muslim Woman Act has come into force.
   Shabana Bano vs. Imran Khan AIR 2010 SC 305
3. **Negligence by Statutory Body:** It was held that even a public authority exercising statutory power is not exempt from liability for negligent actions.
   Municipal Corporation of Delhi vs Uphaar Tragedy Victims Association and Ors. (2011) 14 SCC 481
4. **Right to Porperty:** Right to Property is not a basic feature of the Constitution but is a human right.
   Tukaram Kana Joshi vs MIDC, AIR 2013 SC 565
5. **Land Acquisition:** Acquisition of land by the similar order is not proper. Not to release the land while the land of others is released.
   Usha Stud & Agricultural Farms Pvt. Ltd. vs. State of Haryana
   AIR 2013 SC 1282
6. **Illegal Gratification:** The defence set up against charge of illegal gratification need not be proved beyond resonable doubt. It is enough if it is shown that it is a preponderent possibility.
   Punjabrao vs. State of Maharashtra, AIR 2002 SC 486
7. **Liability of Public Servant:** Where public servant acts malafide in discharge of his functions as public servent, it is high time in the present socio-economic stuation that the public servant is made liable to damages. Common cause vs. Union of India, 1996 (6) SCC 593.

Part X: Miscellaneous Topics

1. **Tribunals in India: Constitutional Provisions:** Tribunals were added in the Constitution by Constitution (Forty-second Amendment) Act, 1976 as Part XIV-A, which has only two Articles viz. 323-A and 323-B. While Article 323-A deals with Administrative Tribunals; Article 323-B deals with tribunals for other matters. In general sense, the 'Tribunals' are not courts of normal jurisdiction, but they have very specific and predefined work area.
2. **Judicial Review:** Judicial review is a type of court proceeding in which a judge reviews the lawfulness of a statute, decision or action made by a public body. Judicial review is a process under which executive or legislative actions are subject to review by the judiciary.
3. **Difference Between Money Bill and Finance Bill:** The fundamental difference between a money bill and finance bill is that a money bill can be introduced in only the lower house of parliament, i.e. Lok Sabha only, finance bill can be introduced in either of the two houses. Although money bill is a type of finance bill, most of the people use them interchangeably, but they differ in terms of their content.
4. **Definition of Money Bill:** Money Bills as the name suggests, are the bills concerned with the provisions solely

dealing with all or any of the matters prescribed in the Article 110 (1). It encompasses matters relating to the levying, abrogation and regulation of taxes, regulation of government borrowing, the protection of Consolidated or Contingency Fund and inflow or outflow of money from any such funds, appropriation of money from Consolidated Fund of India, and so forth. After obtaining the assent of the President of India, the bill introduced in the House of people i.e. Lok Sabha, which is certified as money bill by the Speaker and then passed to Rajya Sabha for the recommendation of amendments. Further, the Rajya Sabha can keep the bill, for a maximum of 14 days, or else it is deemed to be passed by both the Houses. The Lok Sabha has the authority to accept or reject the suggestions given by the Rajya Sabha.

5. **Definition of Finance Bill:** A bill proposed in Lok Sabha every year, just after the declaration of Union Budget for the upcoming year, to undertake the proposals made by the Government, is known as Finance Bill. It refers to any bill that contains matters relating to the revenue and expenditure of the country. It takes into account the imposition of new taxes, alteration in the existing tax structure or continuance of the older one, beyond the term assented by the Parliament are presented via finance bill. A memorandum comprising of explanations of the provisions covered is enclosed with the bill. The bill has to be enacted by the Parliament within 75 days of its introduction. The finance bill is classified into two categories, which is described as under:

   Category A: The bill covers the provisions of Article 110 (1) of the Constitution of India. It can be originated only in Lok Sabha, after the assent of the President of the country.

   Category B: It contains clauses relating to the expenditure from Consolidated Fund of India. Such bills can be introduced in any of the two houses. Prior approval of President is the must, for consideration of the bills.

6. **Article 21 of Constitution & various dimensions added by SC:**

    1. AK Gopalan vs State of Madras: Procedure established by law
    2. Right to have fair procedure- Maneka Gandhi vs UOI
    3. Right to legal Aid- Hussainara vs Home Sec, Bihar
    4. Right to Public Trial- Vineet Narain vs UOI
    5. Right to go abroad- Satwant Singh Sawhney vs Assistant Passport Officer, New Delhi, Maneka Gandhi vs Union of India
    6. Right to privacy-Kharak Singh vs State of U.P
    7. Right against solitary confinement Sunil Batra vs Delhi Administration
    8. Right against hand cuffing Prem Shankar vs Delhi Administration
    9. Right to Medical Care- Parmananda Katara vs Union of India
    10. Right to Health- Consumer Education and Research Centre vs Union of India
    11. Right to Social Security and Protection of Family- L.I.C. of India vs Consumer Education and Research Centre
    12. Right to Shelter- Chameli Singh vs State of U.P
    13. Right To Livelihood- D.T.C. vs D.T.C. Mazdoor Congress
    14. Right to Reputation- D.F. Marion vs Minnie Davis
    15. Right Against Sexual Harassment at Workplace- Vishakha vs State of Rajasthan
    16. Right To Live with Human Dignity- Maneka Gandhi vs Union of India,Francis Coralie vs Union Territory of Delhi
    17. Right against Bar Fetters-Sunil Batra vs Delhi Administration

18. Right to Write a Book-State of Maharashtra vs Prabhakar Pandurang
19. Right against Delayed Execution: Sher Singh vs State of Punjab
20. Right against Public Hanging: Attorney General of India vs Lachma Devi
21. Death by Hanging not Violative of Article 21- Deena vs Union of India
22. Right to Bail: Babu Singh vs State of Uttar Pradesh
23. Right to Fair Trial- Zahira Habibullah Sheikh vs State of Gujarat
24. Right to Speedy Trial- Hussainara Khatoon vs Home Secretary, State of Bihar.
25. Right to Free Legal Aid & Right to Appeal: M.H. Hoskot vs State of Maharashtra
26. Right against Illegal Detention: Joginder Kumar vs State of Uttar Pradesh
27. Disclosure of Dreadful Diseases: Mr. X vs Hospital Z on AIDS, HIV
28. Tapping of Telephone: PUCL vs Union of India
29. Right Against Noise Pollution: In Re: Noise Pollution
30. Murli S. Deora vs Union of India-smoking in public place
31. Right to get Pollution Free Water and Air: Subhas Kumar vs State of Bihar.
32. Euthanasia and Right to Life-Gian Kaur vs State of Punjab
33. Right to Work: Olga Tellis vs BMC
34. Right to Marriage: Mangayakarasi vs M. Yuvaraj
35. Right to Food: PUCL vs UOI
36. Right to Legal Aid: Sheela Barse vs UOI
37. Right to Education: Mohini jain vs State of Karnataka
38. Right to have clean Environment: MC Mehta vs Kermateks UOI
39. Right to have shelter-Chameli vs State

40. Right to receive compensation: Rudal Shah vs State of Bihar

7. **104th Constitution Amendment Act:** The reservation given to SCs, STs and the Anglo-Indian community for the past 70 years was to end on January 25, 2020. The 104th Constitution Amendment Act extends it by 10 years. Reservation to the Scheduled Castes and Scheduled Tribes in the Lok Sabha and the Assemblies.

   The reservation has been included in Article 334 and therefore the bill seeks to amend the Article. Article 334 lays down that the provisions for reservation of seats and special representation of Anglo-Indians, SC and ST will cease after 40 years. The clause was included in 1949. After 40 years, it is being amended with an extension of 10 years. A similar reservation for the Anglo-Indian community in Lok Sabha and State Assemblies is not being extended, as per the provisions of the Act. According to Law Minster, there are only 296 members of the Anglo-Indian community in India.

8. **Section 6A of Indian Citizenship Act 1955:** Section 6A was included in 1986 as an amendment to the Citizenship Act following the Assam Accord of 1985. The amendment gave citizenship to all migrants from Bangladesh who came to Assam before March 25, 1971.

   Those who entered after this date needed to register themselves. Thus, Section 6A pertains only to migrants to Assam.

   Relevant Citizenship provisions in India:

   Part II of the Constitution including Articles 5 to 11 and Indian Citizenship Act 1955 deals exhaustively with provisions relating to citizenship in India.

   Article 6 of the Constitution deals with citizenship of those who migrated to any part of India before July 19, 1948, from territory that had become part of Pakistan.

   Indian Citizenship Act 1955 provides for following ways in which one can become a citizen of India:

Citizenship by Birth

Citizenship by Descent

Citizenship by Registration

Citizenship by Naturalisation (Section 6)

Section 6A was included as an amendment to the Citizenship Act following the Assam Accord of 1985.

9. **Citizenship Amendment Act:** The Act makes illegal migrants who are Hindus, Sikhs, Buddhists, Jains, Parsis and Christians from Afghanistan, Bangladesh and Pakistan, who entered India on or before 31 December 2014, eligible for Indian citizenship.

   The Act relaxes the 11-year requirement for citizenship by naturalization to five years for persons belonging to the same six religions and three countries.

   These provisions of Act will not apply to the tribal areas of Assam, Meghalaya, Mizoram, and Tripura, included in the Sixth Schedule to the Constitution as well as the areas which are regulated through the Inner Line Permit.

   The Act provides that the registration of Overseas Citizen of India (OCI) cardholders may be cancelled if they violate any law notified by the Central government.

   The Union Cabinet cleared the Bill on 4 December 2019. It was passed by the Lok Sabha & Rajyasabha on 10th & 11th December, 2019 respectively.

10. **What is the Citizenship Act 1995?**

    Under Article 9 of the Indian Constitution, a person who voluntarily acquires citizenship of any other country is no longer an Indian citizen.

    Citizenship by descent: Persons born outside India on or after January 26, 1950, but before December 10, 1992, are citizens of India by descent if their father was a citizen of India at the time of their birth.

    From December 3, 2004, onwards, persons born outside of India shall not be considered citizens of India unless their birth is registered at an Indian consulate within one year of the date of birth.

In Section 8 of the Citizenship Act 1955, if an adult makes a declaration of renunciation of Indian citizenship, he loses Indian citizenship.

The first enactment made for dealing with foreigners was the Foreigners Act, 1864, which provided for the expulsion of foreigners and their arrest, detention pending removal, and for a ban on their entry into India after removal.

The Passport (Entry into India) Act, 1920, empowered the Government to make rules requiring persons entering India to be in possession of passports. This rule also granted the Government the power to remove from India any person who entered without a passport.

The Foreigners Act, 1946 empowers the Government to make provisions for regulating the entry of foreigners into India. Its most important provision is that the 'burden of proof' lies with the person, and not with the authorities. This has been upheld by a Constitution Bench of the Supreme Court.

The Foreigners (Tribunals) Order, 1964 empowers District Magistrates in all States and Union Territories to set up tribunals to decide whether a person staying illegally in India is a foreigner or not.

The Illegal Migrants (Determination by Tribunals) Act, 1983 was introduced for the detection and deportation of illegal migrants who had entered India on or after March 25, 1971.

One factor for its failure was that it did not contain any provision on 'burden of proof' similar to the Foreigners Act, 1946.

In 2005, in the Supreme Court not only quashed the IMDT Act but also closed all Tribunals in Assam functioning under the Act. It, then, transferred all pending cases at the IMDT tribunals to the Foreigners Tribunals constituted under the Foreigners (Tribunals) Order, 1964.

11. **Fundamental Rights:**

Part III of the Indian Constitution guarantees six fundamental rights to all the citizens:

(a) Right to Equality (Articles 14–18)
(b) Right to Freedom (Articles 19–22)
(c) Right against Exploitation (Articles 23–24)
(d) Right to Freedom of Religion (Articles 25–28)
(e) Cultural and Educational Rights (Articles 29–30)
(f) Right to Constitutional Remedies (Article 32).

The Fundamental Rights are meant for promoting the idea of political democracy. They are justiciable in nature, that is, they are enforceable by the courts for their violation. Fundamental Rights are not absolute and subject to reasonable restrictions. They can also be suspended during the operation of a National Emergency except the rights guaranteed by Articles 20 and 21.

12. **Composition of Lok Sabha**

Strength of Lok Sabha: Article 81 of the Constitution defines the composition of the House of the People or Lok Sabha.

It states that the House shall not consist of more than 550 elected members of whom not more than 20 will represent Union Territories.

Under Article 331, the President can nominate up to two Anglo-Indians if he/she feels the community is inadequately represented in the House.

At present, the strength of the Lok Sabha is 543, of which 530 have been allocated to the States and the rest to the Union Territories.

The strength of the Lok Sabha hasn't always been 543 seats. Originally, Article 81 provided that the Lok Sabha shall not have more than 500 members. The first House constituted in 1952 had 497.

Criteria of allotting Lok Sabha seats to a state: Article 81 also mandates that the number of Lok Sabha seats allotted to a state would be such that the ratio between that number and the population of the state is, as far as possible, the same for all states. This is to ensure that every state is equally represented.

However, this logic does not apply to small States whose population is not more than 60 lakh. So, at least one seat is allocated to every state even if it means that its population-to-seat-ratio is not enough to qualify it for that seat.

Census considered for population: As per Clause 3 of Article 81, population, for the purpose of allocation of seats, means "population as ascertained at the last preceding census of which the relevant figures have been published". In other words, the last published Census.

But, by an amendment to this Clause in 2003, the population now means population as per the 1971 Census, until the first Census taken after 2026. This was justified on the ground that a uniform population growth rate would be achieved throughout the country by 2026.

13. Tricks to learn Schedules of the Constitution

'TEARS OF OLD PM'

T= Territory (I)

E= Emoluments (II)

A= Affirmations and Oaths (III)

R= Rajya Sabha (IV)

S= Scheduled areas (V)

O= Other Scheduled areas (VI)

F= Federal provisions, 3 lists (VII)

O= Official languages (VIII)

L= Land reforms (IX)

D= Defection (X)

P= Panchayats (XI)

M= Municipalities (XII)

14. Article 341

- Article 341 of the Constitution provides certain privileges and concessions to the members of Scheduled Castes
- Under the provision of Article 341, first list of SCs in relation to a states/UT is to be issued by a notified Order of the President after consulting concerned State Government.
- But the clause (2) of Article 341 envisages that, any subsequent inclusion in or exclusion from the list of Scheduled Castes can be effected through an Act of Parliament.

15. Appointment of CJI: Article 124 of the Constitution of India provides for the manner of appointing judges to the Supreme Court (SC). But there is no specific provision in the Constitution for appointing the Chief Justice.

CJI should be the senior most judge of the Supreme Court (SC). Law Minister is to seek recommendation of the outgoing CJI for appointment of new CJI at an appropriate time.

In case of doubt about the fitness of the senior-most Judge to hold office of CJI, consultation with other Judges under Article 124(2) is to be made.

Law Minister is to put up recommendation to Prime Minister (PM) who will advise the President on appointment.

Seniority at the apex court is determined not by age, but by:

The date a judge was appointed to the SC.

If two judges are elevated to the Supreme Court on the same day, (1) the one who was sworn in first as a judge would trump another; (2) if both were sworn in as judges on the same day, the one with more years of High Court service would 'win' in the seniority stakes; (3) an appointment from the bench would 'trump' in seniority an appointee from the bar.

Tenure: Once appointed, the Chief Justice remains in office until the age of 65 years.

Article 124(4) of Constitution of India provides that a SC Judge including CJI can be moved only through a process of impeachment by Parliament.

16. **Different types of Writs**

Habeas Corpus - to direct the release of a person detained unlawfully.

Mandamus - to direct a public authority to do its duty.

Quo Warranto - to direct a person to vacate an office assumed wrongfully.

Prohibition - to prohibit a lower court from proceeding on a case.

Certiorari - power of the higher court to remove a proceeding from a lower court and bring it before itself.

17. **Foreign Phrases:**

- De facto- By means of fact.
- De hors- Outside the scope of.
- Decree nisi- A conditional decree, not absolute.
- En bloc- All at the same time.
- Eo nomine- By that very name.
- Ex curia- Out of court.
- Fiat accompli- A thing already done.
- Feme sole- An unmarried woman.
- Gratis dictum- Mere assertion.
- Ipse dixit- His mere word.

18. **Maxim:**

- Actus dei nemini facit injuriam
- Actus- action/Act
- Dei- god
- Nemini- towards nobody

- Facit- to do/does
- Injuriam- legal injury/cause
- An Act of god causes legal injury to no one.
- Culpa lata aequiparatur dolo
- Culpa- gross negligence
- Lata- is/can
- Aequi- equal
- Paratur- proportionate
- Aequiparatur- equivalent to
- Dolo- cheat/fraud
- Gross negligence is equivalent to cheat.
- Demissio regis vel coronoe (Transfer of property)
- Furiosi nulla voluntas est (Mad men have no free will)
- De die in diem (From day-to-day)

19. Important Parliamentary Terms:

(a) ACT- A Bill passed by both Houses of Parliament and assented to by the President.

(b) ADJOURNMENT MOTION- It interrupts the normal business of the Houses and draws attention to a matter of grave public importance.

(c) APPROPRIATION BILL- It is a bill containing all the demands for grants voted by Lok Sabha along with Expenditure charged on Consolidated Fund of India.

(d) PLEBISCITE- It is a direct vote of qualified voters in regard to some important public question.

(e) PROROGATION- The termination of the service of House by an order made by the President under Article 85(2)(a).

20. Ad Hoc Commissions-Years And Objectives

1. States Reorganisation Commission - 1955
   - Recommend the reorganization of state boundaries.

2. Kothari Commission - 1964
   - To formulate the general principles and guidelines for the development of education at all levels.
   - To advise the government on a standardized national pattern of education in India.
3. Kapur Commission-1966
   - To inquire into the conspiracy that led to the assassination of Mahatma Gandhi.
4. Khosla Commission-1970
   - To investigate the death of Subhas Chandra Bose in 1945.
5. Mandal Commission - 1980
   - Identified over 450 backward classes comprising 52% of the country's population.
   - Recommended 27% of the seats in academic institutions and jobs in Govt. organisations for these classes.
6. Sarkaria Commission-1983
   - To examine the balance of power between Centre and States and suggest reforms.
   - Gave appropriate recommendations on appointment of Governor.
7. Mukherjee Commission - 1959
   - To investigate the death of Subhas Chandra Bose in 1945.
8. Nanavati Commission-2000
   - To investigate the 1984 anti-Sikh riots.
9. Narendran Commission - 2000
   - Study and report the representation of Backward Classes in the State public services.
10. National Commission to review the working of the Constitution - February 2000

- Suggested changes in the electoral laws, setting up a National Judicial Commission for appointing judges and election of the Prime Minister by Lok Sabha.

21. Legal GK

1. Who was the first Chief Information Commissioner of India?–Wajahat Habibullah
2. The Protection of Women from Domestic Violence Act came into force on: 26th October 2006
3. In which case the Dissolution of Bihar Legislative Assembly by Governor before formation of Government was declared unconstitutional?–Rameshwar Prasad vs U.O.I.
4. 'Law Day' is celebrated in India on: 26th November
5. Newly inserted Chapter XXIA of Criminal Procedure Code deals with Plea Bargaining

Part XI: The Constitutional Amendment Acts

S. No.	Act	Amendment made
1.	The First Amendment Act, 1951	Articles amended—15, 19, 85, 87, 174, 176, 341, 342, 376.
2.	The Second Amendment Act, 1952	Ratified by States.
3.	The Third Amendment Act, 1954	Articles inserted—31A, 31B Schedule added—Ninth Article amended—81 Scheduled amended-Seventh Schedule-List III, Entry 33.
4.	The Fourth Amendment Act, 1955	Articles amended—31, 31A, 305 Schedule amended—Ninth.
5.	The Fifth Amendment Act, 1955	Article amended—3
6.	The Sixth Amendment Act, 1956	Articles amended—269, 286 Schedules amended— Seventh Schedule List-II, Entry 54; List I, Entry 92A inserted.

7.	The Seventh Amendment Act, 1956	Articles amended—49, 80, 81, 82, 131, 153, 158, 168, 170, 171, 216, 217, 220, 222, 224, 230, 231, 232, 239, 240, 298, 371, Articles inserted— 258, 290A, 350A, 350B, 372A, 378A. Schedules amended—First, Second, Fourth, Seventh-List I, Entries 32, 67; List II, Entries 12, 24; List III, Entry 40. Articles omitted—238, 242, 243, 259, 278, 306, 379-391. Schedule omitted—Second, Part-B, consequential amendments in numerous provisions.
8.	The Eighth Amendment Act, 1959	Article 334 amended-20 years substituted for 10 years.
9.	The Ninth Amendment Act, 1960	First Schedule amended—to transfer certain Territories from the States of Assam, Punjab, West Bengal and the Union Territory of Tripura to Pakistan, implementing the Indo-Pakistan agreements of different dates.

10.	The Tenth Amendment Act, 1961	Article 240 and First Schedule amended-to incorporate Dadra and Nagar Haveli as a Union Territory.
11.	The Eleventh Amendment Act, 1961	Articles 66(1) and 71(3) to narrow down grounds for challenging validity of election of President or Vice-President.
12.	The Twelfth Amendment Act, 1962	Article 240 and First Schedule amended—to incorporate Goa, Daman and Diu as a Union Territory.
13.	The Thirteenth Amendment Act, 1962	Article 371 inserted to make special provisions for the administration of the State of Nagaland.
14.	The Fourteenth Amendment Act, 1962	Provided that Pondicherry, Karaikal, Mahe and Yanam, the former French Territories, should be specified in the Constitution as the Union Territory of Pondicherry.
15.	The Fifteenth Amendment Act, 1963	Amends a number of Articles 124, 128, 217, 222, 224, 224A, 226, 297, 311, 316, Entry 78, List I. The more important of these changes are the raising of the age of retirement of a

		High Court Judge from 60 to 62; the extension of the jurisdiction of a High Court to issue writs under Article 226 to a Government or authority situated outside its territorial jurisdiction where the cause of action arises within such jurisdiction; modifying the procedure imposed by Article 311 upon the pleasure of the President or Governor to dismiss a civil servant.
16.	The Sixteenth Amendment Act, 1963	Amends Article 19 to enable the Parliament to make laws providing restrictions upon the freedom of expression questioning the sovereignty or integrity of the Union of India, with consequential changes in Articles 84, 173, Third Schedule.
17.	The Seventeenth Amendment Act, 1964	Amends Article 31A (definition of 'estate' amended with retrospective effect); Entries 21-64 added to the Ninth Schedule.

18.	The Eighteenth Amendment Act, 1966	Adding Explanations to Article 3. Provision was made for the formation of two States, Punjab and Haryana, by reorganizing Punjab on linguistic basis. The explanation added to Article 3, was to clarify that the Parliament has the power to create a new State or Union Territory.
19.	The Nineteenth Amendment Act, 1966	Amending Article 324 to clarify the duties of the Election Commission.
20.	The Twentieth Amendment Act, 1966	Article 233A inserted to validate the appointment of District Judges.
21.	The Twenty-first Amendment Act, 1967	Includes 'Sindhi' in the List of Languages in the Eighth Schedule.
22.	The Twenty-second Amendment Act, 1969	Inserts Articles 244A, 371B and Cl. (1A) in Article 275, to constitute an autonomous State within the State of Assam (Meghalaya) comprising certain areas specified in Part A of the Sixth Schedule.
23.	The Twenty-third Amendment Act, 1970	Amending Articles 330, 332, 333, 334 to extend the period of reservation for Scheduled Castes and Tribes).

24.	The Twenty-fourth Amendment Act, 1970	Inserting Clause (4) in Article 13, amending Article 368 to nullified the effect of Golak Nath case.
25.	The Twenty-fifth Amendment Act, 1971	Clause (2) of Article 31 amended and clause (2A) inserted, Article 31 C inserted. The jurisdiction of the Courts to determine the adequacy of compensation on acquisition of property was taken away. A new clause was added to lay down that no law which declared that it was for giving effect to the principles specified in clauses (b) and (c) of Article 39 would be called in question on the ground that it is inconsistent with the fundamental rights.
26.	The Twenty-sixth Amendment Act, 1971	Omitting Articles 291, 362; inserting Article 363A; amending Article 366 (22). The recognition to the Rulers of Princely States was withdrawn and their privy purses were abolished.

27.	The Twenty-seventh Amendment Act 1971	Amending Articles 239A; inserting Articles 239B; amending Articles 240; inserting Articles 371C. Two new Union Territories viz. Mizoram and Aurnachal Pradesh were formed.
28.	The Twenty-eighth Amendment Act, 1972.	Inserted Articles 312 A; omitting Articles 314. The conditions of service and privileges of former Indian Civil Service officers were abolished.
29.	The Twenty-ninth Amendment Act, 1972	Adding items 65-66 to the Ninth Schedule.
30.	The Thirtieth Amendment Act, 1972	Amending Article 133 (1). Appeals to the Supreme Court were curtailed.
31.	The Thirty-first Amendment Act, 1973.	Amending Articles 81, 330, 332. Elected seats in Lok Sabha increased from 525 to 545.
32.	The Thirty-second Amendment Act, 1973	Amending Articles 371 (1) and inserting Articles 371D-371E amending Entry 63 of List I, Seventh Schedule. The object was to include six provisions in regard to Andhra Pradesh.
33.	The Thirty-third Amendment Act, 1974	Amending Articles 101, 190.

34.	The Thirty-fourth Amendment Act, 1974	Adding items of 67-86 to the Ninth Schedule.
35.	The Thirty-fifth Amendment Act, 1974.	Inserting Article 2A and amending Articles 80-81; adding Tenth Schedule. Sikkim was made an associate State.
36.	The Thirty-sixth Amendment Act, 1975	Omitting Articles 2A, Schedule X; adding item 22 to Schedule I; inserting Article 371 F; adding Entry 22 to Schedule Ivs Sikkim was made a fully-fledged State.
37.	The Thirty-seventh Amendment Act, 1975	Amending Articles 239A-240; repealing tenth Schedule. Provision was made for a Legislative Assembly and Council of Ministers for the Union Territory of Arunachal Pradesh.
38.	The Thirty-eighth Amendment Act, 1975	Amending Articles 123, 213, 239B, 352, 356, 359, 360. Declaration of Emergency by the President and promulgation of Ordinances by the President or Governor made issues over which the judiciary would not be able to exercise its power of review.

39.	The Thirty-ninth Amendment Act, 1975	Amending Article 71; inserting Article 329A. Questions regarding elections of President, Vice-President, Prime Minister and Speaker of Lok Sabha taken out of the purview of the judiciary.
40.	The Fortieth Amendment Act, 1976	Substituting Article 297; adding Entries 125 to 188 to Schedule IX. It was provided that all lands, minerals etc. underlying the ocean within the territorial waters or the continental shelf or the exclusive economic zone of India shall vest in the Union. Power to determine the limits of territorial waters, continental shelf, etc. was vested in the Parliament.
41.	The Forty-first Amendment Act, 1976	Amending Article 316, Upper age for members of State Public Service Commission raised from 60 to 62.
42.	The Forty-second Amendment Act, 1976	Amending Preamble Articles 31 C, 39, 55, 74, 77, 81, 82, 83, 100, 102, 105, 118, 145, 166, 170, 172, 189, 191, 194, 208, 217, 225, 227, 228, 311, 312, 330, 352, 353, 356,

		357, 358, 359, 366, 368, 371 F, Seventh Schedule; Substituting Articles 103, 150, 192, 226; inserting Articles 31 D, 32A, 39A, 43A, 48A, 51A, 131A, 139, 144A, 226A, 228A, 257A, 323A, 323B. This amendment was almost a complete revision of the Constitution and many material changes were incorporated. It was enacted during an Emergency. The next Government that came into power in 1977 repealed most of the amendments.
43.	The Forty-third Amendment Act, 1977	Omitting Articles 31D, 32A, 131A, and 144A; amending Article 145.
44.	The Forty-fourth Amendment Act, 1978	Omitting Articles 19 (1) (f), 31, 77 (4), 123 (4), 166 (4), 213 (4), 239 B (4), 257A, 329 A. Inserting Articles 30 (1A), 134 A, 300A, 361A. Amending and substituting, Articles: 19 (1), 22, 31A, 31C, 38, 71, 74, 83, 103, 105, 123, 132-134, 139A, 172, 192, 194, 217, 225, 226, 227, 329, 352, 356, 358, 359, 360, 361, 371F.

		Cancelling the amendments made by the 42nd Amendment Act to – Articles 100, 102, 105, 118, 191, 194, 208.
		(6 clauses of the Bill were rejected by the Rajya Sabha). The changes made by the 42nd Amendment Act were repealed or altered and the Constitution was brought back in its original form. But the Right to Property was taken away from the Chapter of Fundamental Rights and put as a new Article 300A.
45.	The Forty-fifth Amendment Act, 1980	Extending reservation under Article 334 from 30 to 40 years.
46.	The Forty-sixth Amendment Act, 1982	Amending Articles 269, 286, 366, List I, relating to Sales Tax.
47.	The Forty-seventh Amendment Act, 1984	Adding Entries 189-202, to the Ninth Schedule.
48.	The Forty-eight Amendment Act, 1984	Inserting Proviso to Clause (5) of Article 356 to extend President's Rule in Punjab.
49.	The Forty-ninth Amendment Act, 1984	Amending Article 244, Fifth & Sixth Schedules. Sixth Schedule was made applicable to Tripura.

50.	The Fiftieth Amendment Act, 1984	Substituting Article 33. Its scope was enlarged and many other forces were included in its ambit.
51.	The Fifty-first Amendment Act, 1984	Amending Articles 330, 332.
52.	The Fifty-second Amendment Act, 1985	Amending Articles 101, 102, 190, 191; adding Tenth Schedule (anti-defection). It was declared that a member who defects from his party would become subject to disqualification.
53.	The Fifty-third Amendment Act, 1986	Adding Article 371 G Mizoram was made a State.
54.	The Fifty-fourth Amendment Act, 1986	Amending Articles 125, 221, Second Schedule. Appropriate provisions were made to increase the salary of the judges of the Supreme Court and High Courts.
55.	The Fifty-fifth Amendment Act, 1986	Inserting Article 371-H. State of Arunachal Pradesh was formed.
56.	The Fifty-sixth Amendment Act, 1987	Inserting Article 371-I. The Union Territory of Goa, Daman, and Diu was divided. Goa was made a state and provision for State assemblies were inserted. Daman and Diu to be a Union Territory.

57.	The Fifty-seventh Amendment Act, 1987	Clause (3A) inserted in Article 332, Articles 330 and 332 were amended to make provision for reservation of seats for Scheduled Tribes of Nagaland, Meghalaya, Mizoram and Arunachal Pradesh, in the Lok Sabha and in the legislative assemblies of Nagaland and Meghalaya.
58.	The Constitution (Fifty-eighth Amendment Act, 1987)	Inserting Article 394A. The People had been demanding that the authoritative text of the Constitution should be published in Hindi. This amendment authorised the President to publish the authoritative text of the Constitution in Hindi.
59.	The Fifty-ninth Amendment Act, 1988	Inserting Article 359-A; Amending Article 356. Article 356 was amended to provide that the declaration of Emergency may remain in operation upto 3 years. The amendment made in Article 352 provided that the Emergency with respect to Punjab shall operate only in that State.

60.	The Sixtieth Amendment Act, 1988	Amending Article 276, to increase the limit of profession tax from ₹ 250 to ₹ 2,500.
61.	The Sixty-first Amendment Act, 1989	Amending Article 326, to reduce the voting age from 21 to 18 years.
62.	The Sixty-second Amendment Act, 1989	Amending Article 334, to increase the period of reservation of seats for Scheduled castes and tribes for 10 years i.e. up to the year 2000.A.D.
63.	The Sixty-third Amendment Act, 1989	Amending Article 356 omitting Proviso to Cl. (5) and omitting Article 359 A
64.	The Sixty-fourth Amendment Act, 1990	Amending Article 356. As normalcy could not be restored in Punjab, Emergency was to be continued. For that necessary provision was made in Article 356.
65.	The Sixty-fifth Amendment Act, 1990	Amending Article 338 to provide for a National Commission for Scheduled castes and Scheduled Tribes. The Commission has been given wide powers.
66.	The Sixty-sixth Amendment Act, 1990	Inserting Entries 203 to 257 in the Ninth Schedule.

67.	The Sixty-seventh Amendment Act, 1990	Amending Article 356, 3rd Proviso, clause (a), was extending the period to 5 years.
68.	The Sixty-eighth Amendment Act, 1991	Amending Article 356, 3rd Proviso, clause (a), is extending the period to 5 years.
69.	The Sixty-ninth Amendment Act, 1991	Inserting Articles 239AA and 239AB, to provide for a legislative Assembly and Council of Ministers for the Union Territory of Delhi.
70.	The Seventieth Amendment Act, 1992	Amending Articles 54 and 368 to include members of legislative Assemblies of Union Territories of Delhi and Pondicherry in the electoral college.
71.	The Seventy-first Amendment Act, 1992	Inserting entries 7, 9, 11 and reinserting some entries in 8th Schedule.
72.	The Seventy-second Amendment Act, 1992	Inserting clause (3B) in Article 332.
73.	The Seventy-third Amendment Act, 1992	Part IX, Re-Panchayats from Articles 243 to 243O, Eleventh Schedule.
74.	The Seventy-fourth Amendment Act, 1992	Re. Nagarpalika (Municipalities) Inserting Part IXA, containing Articles 243 P to 243 ZG; Twelfth Schedule.

75.	The Seventy-fifth Amendment Act, 1993	Inserting sub-clause. (h) in Article 323 B (2).
76.	The Seventy-sixth Amendment Act, 1994	Inserting entry 237A, in the 9th Schedule
77.	The Seventy-seventh Amendment Act, 1995	Inserting clause (4A) in Article 16.
78.	The Seventy-eighth Amendment Act, 1995	Further addition of 27 entries to the 9th Schedule to the Constitution.
79.	The Seventy-Ninth Amendment Act, 1999	Substituting "sixty years" for the words "fifty years" in Article 334.
80.	The Eightieth Amendment Act, 1999	Substituting new clauses for Cls. (1) and (2) of Article 269; new Article for Article 270 and omitting Article 272.
81.	The Eighty-first Amendment Act, 2000	Inserting clause (4B) in Article 16.
82.	The Eighty-Second Amendment Act, 2000	Inserting a Proviso to Article 335.
83.	The Eighty-third Amendment Act, 2001	Inserting clause (3A) in Article 243M
84.	The Eighty-fourth Amendment Act, 2001	Substitution of the figure "2026" relating to census in Articles 55, 81, 82, 170, 330 and 332 for the figure "2000"
85.	The Eighty-fifth Amendment Act, 2001	Substitution of certain words in Article 16 (4A) to protect consequential seniority of reserved category retrospectively.

86.	The Eighty-sixth Amendment Act, 2002	Insertion of Article 21A, substitution of Article 45 and insertion of Article 51A (k).
87.	The Eighty-seventh Amendment) Act, 2003	Substitution of the figure "2001" relating to census in Articles 81, 82, 170 and 330 for the figure "1991."
88.	The Eighty-eighth Amendment Act, 2003	Insertion of Article 268A, substitution of the words, figures and letter "Articles 268, 268A and 269" for the words and figures "Articles 268 and 269" in Article 270 and insertion of Entry "92C" in Union List.
89.	The Eighty-ninth Amendment Act, 2003	Amendment of Article 338 and insertion of Article 338A.
90.	The Ninetieth Amendment Act, 2003	Insertion of a proviso to Article 332 (6).
91.	The Ninety-first amendment Act, 2003	Amendment of Articles 75, 164 and Sch. X, insertion of Article 361B.
92.	The Ninety-second amendment Act, 2003	Addition of "Bodo" "Dogri", "Maithilli" and "Santhali" languages in schedule VIII.
93.	The Ninety-third amendment Act, 2005	Insertion of clause (5) in Article 15.

94.	The Ninety-fourth Amendment Act, 2006	Amendment of Article 164.
95.	The Ninety-fifth Amendment Act, 2009	Amendment of Article 334.
96.	The Ninety-Sixth Amendment Act, 2011	Amendment of Eight Schedules.
97.	The Ninety-seventh Amendment Act, 2011	Amendment of Article 19 insertion of Article 43B, insertion of Part IXB consisting of Articles 243ZH to 243ZT regarding Co-operative Societies.
98.	The Ninety-eighth Amendment Act, 2012	Insertion of New Article 371
99.	The Ninety-ninth Amendment Act, 2014	Insertion of Articles 124A, 124B, 124C Amendments of Articles 124, 127, 128, 217, 222, 224, 224A, 231
100.	The Hundredth Amendment Act, 2015	Amendment to Schedule 1 with regard to States of Assam, West Bengal, Meghalaya and Tripura.
101.	The One Hundredth and First Amendment Act, 2017	Introduced a National Goods and Services Tax in India from 1st July, 2017

102.	The One Hundred and Second Amendment Act, 2018 .	Insertion of Articles 338B, 342A, and added Clause 26C Modification of Articles 338, 366. For appointment of the Nationl commission for Backward Classes.
103.	The One Hundred and Third Amendment Act, 2019	Amendment to Article 15, added clause (6). Amendment to Article 16, added clause (6) For reservation for the advancement of any economically weaker sections of citizens to a maximum of 10% including admissions in educational institution except in the minority institutions.
104.	The One Hundred and Fourth Amendment Act, 2020.	Amendment in Article 334. Extension of reservation from "seventy years" to "eighty years".
105.	The One Hundred and Fifth Amendment Act, 2021.	Amendment in Article 338B, 342A and 366 to restore states' power to make their own OBC lists annulling Supreme Court judgement of 11th May, 2021 in the case, Dr. Laxmirao Patil vs Chief Minister, Maharashtra.

Appendix-1: List of Additional Landmark Judgments of Supreme Court

S. No.	Related with	Case
1.	Freedom of speech	Romesh Thappar vs State of Madras (1950)
2.	Preventive Detention Act, 1950	AK Gopalan vs State of Madras (1950)
3.	Pre-censorship of media	Brij Bhushan and Another vs State of Delhi (1950)
4.	Caste-based reservation in admission to the educational institutions	State of Madras vs Smt. Champakam Dorairajan (1951)
5.	Power of the Parliament to amend fundamental Rights	Shankari Prasad vs Union of India (1951)
6.	The test of essential religious practices	The Commissioner, Hindu Religious Endowments, Madras vs Sri Lakshmindra Thirtha Swamiar of Shirur Mutt (1954)
7.	Right to privacy	M. P. Sharma and Others vs Satish Chandra (1954)
8.	Pardoning power of the Governor; Jury trial	K. M. Nanavati vs State of Maharashtra (1959)
9.	Cession of a part of the territory of India; Exchange of enclaves with Pakistan	Berubari Union vs Unknown (1960)
10.	Whether privacy is a guaranteed constitutional right?	Kharak Singh vs State of UP and Others (1962)
11.	Power of the Parliament to amend the Constitution	Sajjan Singh vs State of Rajasthan (1965)

12.	Power of the Parliament to amend Fundamental Rights under Part III of the Constitution	L. C. Golaknath and Others vs State of Punjab and Others (1967)
13.	Abolition of privy purse by the presidential order	H. H. Maharajadhiraja Madhav Rao Jiwaji Rao Scindia vs Union of India (1970)
14.	Power of the Parliament to amend the Constitution; The "Doctrine of Basic Structure"	Kesavananda Bharati vs State of Kerala (1973)
15.	Election of Indira Gandhi; Election malpractice	Indira Nehru Gandhi vs Raj Narain (1975)
16.	Right to move writ petitions before High Courts under Article 226, during the Emergency	ADM Jabalpur vs Shivkant Shukla (1976)
17.	Personal liberty under Article 21; "Procedure established by law" and "Due process of law"	Maneka Gandhi vs Union of India (1978)
18.	The rights of the under trial prisoners	Hussainara Khatoon and Others vs Home Secretary, State of Bihar (1979)
19.	Capital punishment (death penalty); the doctrine of "rarest of rare case"	Bachan Singh vs State of Punjab (1980)
20.	Harmony and balance between fundamental rights and directive principles	Minerva Mills Ltd. vs Union of India (1980)
21.	Appointment of judges of the Supreme Court and High Courts	S. P. Gupta vs President of India and Others (1981)

22.	Whether a person to whom legal injury is caused by reason of violation of a fundamental right is unable to approach the court, any member of the public acting bona fide can move the court for relief under Article 32 and Article 226?	Bandhua Mukti Morcha vs Union of India (1984)
23.	Freedom of press under freedom of speech and expression	Indian Express Newspapers vs Union of India and Others (1984)
24.	Providing maintenance to a divorced Muslim woman	Mohd. Ahmad Khan vs Shah Bano Begum and Others (1985)
25.	Re-Promulgation of ordinances	Dr. D. C. Wadhwa and Others vs State of Bihar and Others (1986)
26.	Responsibility of industries in an accident; compensation; scope and ambit of the jurisdiction of the Supreme Court under Article 32	M. C. Mehta vs Union of India and Others (1986)
27.	Whether forcing the children to sing the national anthem violated their fundamental right to religion?	Bijoe Emmanuel and Others vs State of Kerala and Others (1986)
28.	Pardoning power of the President	Kehar Singh and Another vs Union of India and Another (1988)
29.	Right to education	Mohini Jain vs State of Karnataka (1989)

30.	Reservation for backward classes in Government jobs	Indira Sawhney and Others vs Union of India (1992)
31.	The constitutional validity of Anti-defection law	Kihoto Hollohan vs Zachillhu and Others (1992)
32.	Appointment of judges of the Supreme Court and High Courts	Advocate on Record Association vs Union of India (1993)
33.	Right to education	Unni Krishnan, J. P. and Others vs State of Andhra Pradesh and Others (1993)
34.	Proclamation of Emergency under Article 356 of the Constitution	S. R. Bommai vs Union of India (1994)
35.	Freedom of speech and expression - right to publish autobiography	R. Rajagopal vs State of Tamil Nadu (1994)
36.	Principles against the practice of solemnizing second marriage by conversion to Islam, with first marriage not being dissolved	Sarla Mudgal and Others vs Union of India (1995)
37.	Forest Conservation	T. N. Godavarman Thirumulkpad vs Union of India and Others (1996)
38.	Whether rape is violative of Right to Life under Article 21?	Bodhisattwa Gautam vs Subhra Chakraborty (1996)
39.	Sexual harassment at the workplace; the Supreme Court laid down Vishaka guidelines	Vishakha and Others vs State of Rajasthan (1997)

40.	Curbing political influence in the functioning of the CBI	Vineet Narain and Others vs Union of India (1997)
41.	Power of High Courts and the Supreme Court to review the legislative action	L. Chandra Kumar vs Union of India and Others (1997)
42.	Granting of mining licenses in the scheduled area to non-tribals	Samatha vs State of Andhra Pradesh (1997)
43.	Appointment of judges of the Supreme Court and High Courts	Special Reference case of 1998
44.	Right to food	People's Union For Civil Liberty vs Union of India (2001)
45.	Rights of minority educational institutions	T. M. A. Pai Foundation and Others vs State of Karnataka and Others (2002)
46.	Right to know about public functionaries and candidates for office	Union of India vs Association for Democratic Reforms and Another (2002)
47.	Right of the voters to know about the candidates contesting the election	People's Union of Civil Liberties vs Union of India and Another (2003)
48.	Section 118 of the Indian Succession Act; Advocated a Common Civil Code for the cause of national integration	John Vallamattom and Another vs Union of India (2003)

49.	Reservation policy-on minority and non-minority unaided private colleges, including professional colleges	P. A. Inamdar and Others vs State of Maharashtra and Others (2005)
50.	Police reforms	Prakash Singh and Others vs Union of India and Others (2006)
51.	Reservations in promotions for Scheduled Caste and Scheduled Tribe employees	M. Nagaraj and Others vs Union of India (2006)
52.	Disqualification on the ground of office of profit	Jaya Bachchan vs Union of India and Others (2006)
53.	Requirement of "domicile" in the State concerned for getting elected to the Council of States; Principle of Federalism is a basic structure of the Constitution	Kuldip Nayar vs Union of India and Others (2006)
54.	Interpretation of the doctrine of basic structure of the Constitution; Ninth Schedule is not immunized from the judicial review of the Constitution	I. R. Coelho (Dead) By Lrs vs State of Tamil Nadu and Others (2007)
55.	Reservations to OBCs in central educational institutions	Ashoka Kumar Thakur vs Union of India and Others (2008)

56.	Recognition of passive euthanasia-permitted withdrawal of life-sustaining treatment from patients not in a position to make an informed decision	Aruna Ramchandra Shanbaug vs Union of India and Others (2011)
57.	Settlements and quashing of criminal proceedings	Gian Singh vs State of Punjab (2012)
58.	Court repeated the Vishaka guidelines (1997) and stressed additional measures for their enforcement	Medha Kotwal Lele and Others vs Union of India and Others (2012)
59.	Disqualifications for membership of Parliament and State Legislatures, if convicted of any offence and sentenced to imprisonment for not less than two years	Lily Thomas vs Union of India and Others (2013)
60.	Professionalizing the bureaucracy, promoting efficiency and good governance	T. S. R. Subramanian and Others vs Union of India and Others (2013)
61.	Section 377 of the Indian Penal Code, which criminalized homosexuality	Suresh Kumar Koushal and Another vs Naz Foundation and Others (2013)
62.	Rights of the members of transgender community in India	National Legal Services Authority vs Union of India (2014)
63.	Whether the right to adopt and to be adopted is a fundamental right under Part-III of the Constitution?	Shabnam Hashmi vs Union of India and Others (2014)

64.	The constitutionality of the criminal offence of defamation	Subramaniam Swamy vs Union of India (2014)
65.	The constitutional validity of the RTI Act	Pramati Educational and Cultural Trust vs Union of India and Others (2014)
66.	Fundamental right of free speech and expression; whether the Section 66A of IT Act, 2000 is unconstitutional?	Shreya Singhal vs Union of India (2015)
67.	The constitutional validity of National Judicial Appointments Commission (NJAC) Act	Supreme Court Advocates-on-Record Association and Another vs Union of India (2015)
68.	Right to vote and contest election	Rajbala and Others vs State of Haryana and Others (2015)
69.	Triple Talak or talaq-e-bidat	Shayara Bano vs Union of India and Others (2016)
70.	Whether asking for votes in elections in the name of religion, caste or community will amount to corrupt practice?	Abhiram Singh vs C. D. Commachen (2017)
71.	Re-Promulgation of ordinances against the spirit of constitutionalism	Krishna Kumar Singh and Another vs State of Bihar and Others (2017)
72.	Whether the right to privacy is a fundamental right?	Justice K. S. Puttaswamy (Retd) and Another vs Union of India and Others (2017)

73	The exception to the Marital Rape; whether sex with minor wife is rape?	Independent Thought vs Union of India (2017)
74.	Directions To prevent misuse of Section 498A of the IPC	Rajesh Sharma and Others vs State of UP (2017)
75.	Whether the right to die with dignity is a fundamental right?	Common Cause (A Regd. Society) vs Union of India (2018)
76.	Guidelines against mob lynching	Tehseen S. Poonawalla vs Union of India and Others (2018)
77.	Power tussle between Delhi Government and Lt. Governor	Government of NCT of Delhi vs Union of India (2018)
78.	Directions to prevent misuse of SC/STAct	Dr. Subhash Kashinath Mahajan vs State of Maharashtra (2018)
79.	Right of a girl to marry a person of her own choice	Shafin Jahan vs Asokan K. M. (2018)
80.	The entry of women aged between 10 and 50 to the Sabarimala temple in Kerala	Indian Young Lawyers Association vs State of Kerala (2018)
81.	Section 497 of the Indian Penal Code which criminalized adultery	Joseph Shine vs Union of India (2018)
82.	Section 377 of the IPC, which criminalizes homosexuality	Navtej Singh Johar and Others vs Union of India (2018)
83.	The reservation in promotion for the SC/ST communities	Jarnail Singh and Others vs Lachhmi Narain Gupta and Others (2018)

84.	Ram Janmabhoomi-Babri Masjid land title case	M. Ismail Faruqui and Others vs Union of India and Others (2018)
85.	The constitutional validity of Aadhaar; The Aadhaar Act 2016	Justice Puttaswamy (Retd) and Another vs Union of India and Others (2018)
86.	Honour Killings	Shakti Vahini vs Union of India (2018)
87.	Legislators practicing as advocates	Ashwini Kumar Upadhyay vs Union of India (2018)
88.	Video recording or live streaming of the court proceedings in public interest	Swapnil Tripathi vs Supreme Court of India (2018)
89.	Reservations in promotions for SCs/STs and issues of seniority	B. K. Pavitra vs Union of India (2019)
90.	The implementation of the Forest Rights Act (FRA) of 2006	Wildlife First vs Ministry of Environment and Forest (2019)

Appendix-2: Conflict Areas vs Judgments

S. No.	Conflict Area	Judgments
1.	Freedom of speech and expression	❖ Romesh Thappar vs State of Madras (1950) ❖ Brij Bhushan and Another vs State of Delhi (1950) ❖ Virendra vs State of Punjab (1957) ❖ Hamdard Dawakhana vs Union of India and Others (1959) ❖ Bennett Coleman & Co. and Others vs Union of India and Others (1972) ❖ Indian Express Newspapers vs Union of India and Others (1984) ❖ R Rajagopal vs State of Tamil Nadu (1994) ❖ People's Union for Civil Liberties vs Union of India (2004) ❖ Shreya Singhal vs Union of India (2015)
2.	Reservation in admission to the educational institutions and employment	❖ State of Madras vs Smt. Champakam Dorairajan (1951) ❖ MR Balaji vs State of Mysore (1963) ❖ Indira Sawhney and others vs Union of India (1992) ❖ T. M. A. Pai Foundation and Others vs State of Karnataka and Others (2002)

		❖ P. A. Inamdar and Others vs State of Maharashtra and Others (2005) ❖ M. Nagaraj and Others vs Union of India (2006) ❖ Ashoka Kumar Thakur vs Union of India and Others (2008) ❖ Jarnail Singh and Others vs Lachhmi Narain Gupta and Others (2018) ❖ B. K. Pavitra vs Union of India (2019)
3.	Power of the Parliament to Amend the Constitution	❖ Shankari Prasad vs Union of India (1951) ❖ Sajjan Singh vs State of Rajasthan (1965) ❖ L. C. Golaknath and Others vs State of Punjab and Another (1967) ❖ Kesavananda Bharati vs State of Kerala (1973) ❖ Indira Nehru Gandhi vs Raj Narain and Another (1975) ❖ Minerva Mills Ltd. vs Union of India (1980) ❖ L. Chandra Kumar vs Union of India and Others (1997)
4.	Test of Essential Religious Practices	❖ The Commissioner, Hindu religious endowments, Madras vs Sri Lakshmindra Thirtha Swamiar of Shirur Mutt (1954) ❖ Durgah Committee, Ajmer vs Syed Hussain Ali and Others (1961)

		❖ Sardar Syedna Taher Saifuddin vs State of Bombay (1962) ❖ S. P. Mittal vs Union of India and Others (1982) ❖ Commissioner of Police and Others vs Acharya Jagdishwarananda (2004) ❖ Shayara Bano vs Union of India and Others (2017) ❖ Indian Young Lawyers Association vs State of Kerala (2018)
5.	Right to Privacy	❖ M. P. Sharma and Others vs Satish Chandra (1954) ❖ Kharak Singh vs State of UP and Others (1962) ❖ Justice K. S. Puttaswamy (Retd) and Another vs Union of India and Others (2017)
6.	Basic structure of the Constitution	❖ Kesavananda Bharati vs State of Kerala (1973) ❖ Indira Nehru Gandhi vs Raj Narain and Another (1975) ❖ Minerva Mills Ltd. vs Union of India (1980)
7.	Right to Life and Personal Liberty	❖ Maneka Gandhi vs Union of India (1978) ❖ Sunil Batra vs Delhi Administration (1979) ❖ Hussainara Khatoon and Others vs State of Bihar (1979) ❖ D. K. Basu vs State of West Bengal (1996)

		❖ Vishakha and Others vs State of Rajasthan (1997) ❖ Justice K. S. Puttaswamy (Retd) and Another vs Union of India and Others (2017)
8.	Capital Punishment	❖ Jagmohan Singh vs State of Uttar Pradesh (1973) ❖ Rajendra Prasad vs State of Uttar Pradesh (1979) ❖ Bachan Singh vs State of Punjab (1980) ❖ Machhi Singh and Others vs State of Punjab (1983) ❖ T.vs Vatheeswaran vs State of Tamil Nadu (1983) ❖ Shashi Nayar vs Union of India (1991) ❖ Aloke Nath Dutta vs State of West Bengal (2007) ❖ Swamy Shraddhananda vs State of Karnataka (2008) ❖ Santosh Kumar Satishbhushan Bariyar vs State of Maharashtra (2009) ❖ Shatrughan Chauhan vs Union of India (2014)
9.	Appointment of Judges of the Supreme Court and High Courts	❖ S. P. Gupta vs President of India and Others (1981) ❖ Advocate on Record Association vs Union of India (1993) ❖ Special Reference case of 1998 ❖ Supreme Court Advocates-on-Record- Association and Another vs Union of India (2015)

10.	Re-promulgation of Ordinances	❖ Dr. D. C. Wadhwa and Others vs State of Bihar and Others (1986) ❖ Krishna Kumar Singh and Another vs State of Bihar and Others (2017)
11.	Pardoning power of the President/ Governor	❖ K. M. Nanavati vs State of Maharashtra (1959) ❖ Maru Ram vs Union of India and Another (1980) ❖ Kehar Singh and Another vs Union of India and Another (1988) ❖ Dhananjay Chatterjee Alias Dhana vs State of West Bengal (1994) ❖ Swaran Singh vs State of Uttar Pradesh and Others (1998) ❖ Epuru Sudhakar and Another vs Government of A.P. and Others (2006)
12.	Right to Education	❖ Mohini Jain vs State of Karnataka (1989) ❖ Unni Krishnan, J. P. and Others vs State of Andhra Pradesh and Others (1993) ❖ Pramati Educational & Cultural Trust vs Union of India and Others (2014)
13.	Disqualification of Legislators	❖ Kihoto Hollohan vs Zachillhu and Others (1992) ❖ Ravi S. Naik vs Union of India (1994)

		❖ G. Viswanathan vs Speaker Tamil Nadu Legislative Assembly (1996) ❖ Jaya Bachchan vs Union of India and Others (2006) ❖ Rajendra Singh Rana vs Swami Prasad Maurya and Others (2007) ❖ Speaker Haryana Vidhan Sabha vs Kuldeep Bishnoi and Others (2012)
14.	Proclamation of Emergency under Article 356	❖ State of Rajasthan vs Union of India (1977) ❖ Minerva Mills Ltd. vs Union of India (1980) ❖ S. R. Bommai vs Union of India (1994) ❖ Rameshwar Prasad and Others vs Union of India and Another (2006)
15.	Electoral Reforms	❖ Association for Democratic Reforms vs 'Union of India and Another' (2003) ❖ People's Union of Civil Liberties vs Union of India and Another (2003) ❖ Lily Thomas vs Union of India and Others (2013) ❖ Abhiram Singh vs C. D. Commachen (2017) ❖ Lok Prahari vs Union of India (2018)
16.	Euthanasia	❖ Aruna Ramchandra Shanbaug vs Union of India and Others (2011)

		❖ Common Cause (A Regd. Society) vs Union of India (2018)
17.	Sexual harassment at the workplace	❖ Vishakha and Others vs State of Rajasthan (1997) ❖ Medha Kotwal Lele and Others vs Union of India and Others (2012)
18.	Section 377/ Homosexuality	❖ Suresh Kumar Koushal and Another vs Naz Foundation and Others (2013) ❖ Navtej Singh Johar and Others vs Union of India (2018)
19.	Right to Vote and Contest Elections	❖ Javed and Others vs State of Haryana and Others (2003) ❖ People's Union of Civil Liberties vs Union of India and Another (2003) ❖ Rajbala and Others vs State of Haryana and Others (2015)
20.	Right to Livelihood/ Food	❖ Olga Tellis and Others vs Bombay Municipal Corporation (1985) ❖ Chameli Singh and Others vs State of Uttar Pradesh and Another (1995) ❖ People's Union For Civil Liberty vs Union of India (2001)
21.	Protection of Environment	❖ M.C. Mehta vs Union of India (1982, 1988 & 1998) ❖ Vellore Citizens' Welfare Forum vs Union of India (1995) ❖ T. N. Godavarman Thirumulpad vs Union of India and Others (1996) ❖ Indian Council for Enviro-legal Action vs Union of India and Others (1996)

		❖ Andhra Pradesh Pollution Control Board vs M. vs Nayudu (1999)
22.	Tribal Rights	❖ Samatha vs State of A.P. and Others (1997) ❖ Wildlife First vs Ministry of Environment and Forests (2019)
23.	Fundamental Rights vs Directive Principles of State Policy	❖ State of Madras vs Smt. Champakam Dorairajan (1951) ❖ The Kerala Education Bill vs Unknown (1958) ❖ L. C. Golaknath and Others vs State of Punjab and Another (1967) ❖ Kesavananda Bharati vs State of Kerala (1973) ❖ Minerva Mills Ltd. vs Union of India (1980) ❖ Waman Rao and Others vs Union of India and Others (1980)
24.	Center-State Relations	❖ State of West Bengal vs Union of India (1962) ❖ State of Punjab vs Sat Pal Dang and Others (1968) ❖ State of Rajasthan vs Union of India (1977) ❖ Pradeep Jain vs Union of India (1984) ❖ S. R. Bommai vs Union of India (1994) ❖ Rameshwar Prasad and Others vs Union of India and Another (2006)

Appendix-3:

Change of Rulings of the Supreme Court

When the Supreme Court Judgments Year-wise were held no longer good law, overruled, reversed, doubted or dissented.

1950

AIR 1950 SC 222 held no longer good law in view of AIR 1967 SC 1269 as interpreted in AIR 1969 Cal. 397.

AIR 1950 SC 27 overruled in AIR 1970 SC 564.

AIR 1950 SC 27 overruled in AIR 1973 SC 1425.

1951

AIR 1951 SC 41 dissented in AIR 1954 SC 199.

AIR 1951 SC 97 held no longer good law in AIR 1962 SC 1563.

AIR 1951 SC 97 not followed in AIR 1966 SC 619.

AIR 1951 SC 318 not followed in AIR 1988 SC 520.

1952

AIR 1952 SC 252 dissented in AIR 1954 SC 119.

AIR 1952 SC 192 held not good law in view of Amdt., as interpreted in AIR 5970 Raj. 216.

AIR 1952 SC 252 held no longer good law in view of AIR 1970 SC 564 in AIR 1978 SC 803.

AIR 1952 SC 343 overruled in AIR 1996 SC 1491.

1953

AIR 1953 SC 252 dissented in AIR 1953 SC 333

AIR 1953 SC 108 overruled in AIR 1958 SC 532.

AIR 1953 SC 108 held overruled in AIR 1962 SC 1916.

AIR 1953 SC 252 held overruled by AIR 1955 SC 661.

AIR 1953 SC 221 not applied in AIR 1967 SC 344.

AIR 1953 SC 420 held overruled by AIR 1962 SC 130 in AIR 1980 SC 559.

1954

AIR 1954 SC 636 overruled in AIR 1959 SC 395.

AIR 1954 SC 92 held not good law after the Constitution Amendment Act of 1955 in AIR 1964 Guj. 82.

AIR 1954 SCI 19 held not good law after Constitutional 4th Amdt. Act, 1955-AIR 1964 Guj. 82.

AIR 1954 SC 447 overruled in AIR 1964 SC 1043.

AIR 1954 SC 728 held not good law after Constitution 4th Amdt. Act, 1955 in AIR 1964 Guj. 82.

AIR 1954 SC 513 overruled in AIR 1965 SC 669.

AIR 1954 SC 545 not applied in AIR 1965 AP 196.

AIR 1954 SC 20 held not correct in AIR 1966 SC 1135.

AIR 1954 SC 170 held overruled by AIR 1969 SC 634 as interpreted in AIR 1970 Cal. 15.

AIR 1954 SC 236 not followed in view of later decision in AIR 1968 SC 218 as interpreted in AIR 1971 Cal. 219.

AIR 1954 SC 179 held no good law in view of introduction of S. 5A o COFEPOSA Act - AIR 1987 SC 1748.

AIR 1954 SC 300, overruled- AIR 2017 SC 4161(A)

1955

AIR 1955 SC 781 held overruled by AIR 1959 SC 648 in AIR 1961 Mys. 3.

AIR 1955 SC 3 held no longer good law in AIR 1962 SC 1583.

AIR 1955 SC 41 held no longer good law (after Amdt.) in AIR 1962 ASH 521.

AIR 1955 SC 3 not A followed in AIR 1966 SC 619.

AIR 1955 SC 309 doubted in AIR 1966 SC 220.

AIR 1955 SC 765 held did not apply in AIR 1963 SC 1237.

AIR 1955 SC 41 overruled in AIR 1970 SC 546.

AIR 1955 SC 468 not good law in view of AIR 1967 SC 1030 and 1032 in AIR 1982 Del. 332.

1956

AIR 1956 SC 476 not followed in AIR 1959 SC 1310.

AIR 1956 SC 246 not followed in AIR 1964 Manipur 46.

1957

AIR 1957 SC 13 not followed in AIR 1959 SC 1310.

AIR 1957 SC 95 held not good law after amendment of Industrial Disputes Act, 1947 (14 of 1947) by Act: 18 of 1957 in AIR 1961 Punj. 232.

AIR 1957 SC 121 held no good law after aindt of I.D. Act of 1947 by Act 18 of 1957 in AIR 1961 Punj. 232.

AIR 1957 SC 790 overruled in AIR l962 SC 1621.

AIR 1957 SC 790 held not valid law in AIR 1963 SC 734a.

1958

AIR 1958 SC 468 held overruled by AIR l959 SC 648 in AIR 1961 Mys. 3.

AIR 1958 SC 731, overruled in AIR 2006 SC 212.

AIR 1958 SC 947 dissented in AIR 1968 SC 384.

AIR 1958 SC 947 held no longer good law in view of AIR 1968 SC 384 as interpreted in AIR 1972 Del. 281.

AIR 1958 SC 947 held no longer good law in view of AIR 1968 SC 384 as interpreted in AIR 1973 Del. 24.

AIR 1958 SC 441 not followed in view of changed interpretation of law in (1966) 1 A1I.E.R 524, in AIR 1974 M.P. 88.

AIR 1958 SC 1036 overruled in AIR 199 SC 10.

1959

AIR 1959 SC 847 overruled in AIR 1962 SC 195.

AIR 1959 SC 93 overruled in AIR 1965 SC 669.

AIR 1959 SC 257 overruled in AIR- 1967 : SC 230.

Observations to the contrary in AIR 1959 SC 244 dissented in AIR 1975 1 SC 2291.

1960

AIR 1960 SC 845 overruled in AIR 1966 SC 644.

AIR 1960 SC 1355 overruled in AIR 1967 SC 997.

AIR 1960 SC 131 overruled in AIR 1969 SC 604.

AIR 1960 SC 1203 overruled in AIR 1970 SC 564.

1961

AIR 1961 SC 232 73 disapproved in AIR 1962 SC 1406.

AIR 1961 SC 448 of overruled in AIR 2006 of SC 212.

AIR 1961 SC 736 held no longer good law in view of the Amdt. in AIR 1965 Guj. 105.

AIR 1961 SC 1717 held no longer good law in view of the Amdt. in AIR 1965 Guj. 105.

AIR 1961 SC 58 overruled in AIR 1966 SC 1614.

AIR 1961 SC 1425 doubted in AIR 1966 SC 573.

AIR 1961 SC 808 held no longer good law in view of AIR 1966 SC 470 as interpreted in AIR 1968 Raj. 1.

AIR 1961 SC 610 overruled in AIR 1970 SC 1407.

AIR 1961 SC 4 overruled in AIR 1978 SC 1296.

AIR 1961 SC 884 held no longer good law in view of new Cr.P.C. (1974) in AIR 1981 SC 2198.

AIR 1961 SC 1449 overruled in AIR 1984 SC 1004.

AIR 1961 SC 232 overruled -AIR 2016 SC 5617 (A)

1962

AIR 1962 SC 673 dissented in AIR 1967 SC 1286.

(1962) 46 ITR 609 SC held overruled by AIR 1968 SC 623 as interpreted in AIR 1969 AP 441.

(1962) ITR 609 SC overruled in AIR 1968 SC 623.

AIR 1962 SC 1080 overruled in AIR 1978 SC 548.

AIR 1962 SC 36 overruled in AIR 1993 SC 477.

AIR 1962 SC 1406, overruled in AIR 2016 SC 5617(A)

1963

AIR 1963 SC 548 doubted in AIR 1965 SC 1942.

AIR 1963 SC 1356 not applied in AIR 1965 AP 196.

(1963) 48 ITR SC 177 held no longer good law in view of the Amdt. in AIR 1965 Guj. 105.

AIR 1963 SC 354 overruled in AIR 1966 SC 538.

AIR 1963 SC 358 dissented in AIR 1966 SC 538.

AIR 1963 SC 1207 overruled in AIR 1978 SC 449.

AIR 1963 SC 1873 overruled in AIR 1978 SC 548.

AIR 1963 SC 120 overruled in AIR 1979 SC 1745.

AIR 1963 SC 1681 deemed no longer good in view of the Amdt. of S. 80 of the Railways Act, 1961 in AIR 1981 Del. 135.

AIR 1963 SC 996 held to be obiter in AIR 1992 SC 248.

AIR 1963 SC 649 overruled in AIR 1993 SC 477.

AIR 1963 SC 996 no longer good law in AIR 1995 SC 2348.

AIR 1963 SC 1295, overruled in AIR 2017 SC 4161 (A)

1964

1964 (1) Lab.L.J. 333 dissented in AIR 1964 SC 1617.

AIR 1964 SC 1873 overruled in AIR 1966 SC 1738.

Crl. Appeal 21/1960 dated 14.9.1964 SC held not correct in AIR 1966 SC 1135.

AIR 1964 SC 497 no longer good law in view of Amdt. in S. 115 C.P.C. by 1976 Act - AIR 1993 Pat. 122.

AIR 1964 SC 179 overruled in AIR 1993 SC 477.

1965

AIR 1965 SC 1510 dissented-distinguished in AIR 1969 Ker. 205.

AIR 1965 SC 190 held overruled in AIR 1969 SC 634 as interpreted in AIR 1970 Cal. 15.

Observations in AIR 1965 SC 1017 held obiter and dissented in AIR 1969 SC 634 as interpreted in AIR 1970 Cal. 15.

AIR 1965 SC 101 overruled in AIR 1979 SC 1745.

AIR 1965 SC 414 not followed in AIR 1976 SC 2229 in AIR 1979 Bom. 89.

AIR 1965 SC 414 not followed in view of AIR 1976 SC 2229 in AIR 1982 AP 227.

AIR 1965 SC 1874 not followed in view of AIR 1963 SC 1516 in AIR 1984 Punj. 223.

AIR 1965 SC 1039 not followed in view of AIR 1983 SC 1086, AIR 1984 SC 1026 and AIR 1986 SC 494 in AIR 1989 AP 235.

AIR 1965 SC 414 overruled in AIR 1976 SC 229 as stated in AIR 2003 SC 229.

AIR 1965 SC 183, overruled in AIR 2017 SC 401(B)

1966

AIR 1966 SC 91 overruled in AIR 1967 SC 1507.

AIR 1966 SC 671 held overruled by AIR 1967 SC 1606 as interpreted in AIR 1971 SC 862.

AIR 1966 SC 671 held overruled in AIR 1967 SC 1606 as interpreted in AIR 1971 All. 54.

AIR 1966 SC 1250 overruled in AIR 1972 SC 1880.

AIR 1966 SC 1335 overruled in AIR 1967 SC 1507.

AIR 1966 SC 671 held overruled by AIR 1967 SC 1606 as interpreted in AIR 1971 SC 862.

AIR 1966 SC 671 held overruled in AIR 1967 SC 1606 as interpreted in AIR 1971 All. 54.

AIR 1966 SC 1250 overruled in AIR 1972 SC 1880.

AIR 1966 SC 740 held not good law in view of introduction of S. 5A of COFEPOSA Act in 1987 SC 1748.

AIR 1966 SC 38 held obiter in AIR 2003 SC 2084.

AIR 1966 SC 1686, overruled in AIR 2016 SC 5617(M)

1967

(1967) 2 SCR 949 overruled in AIR 1970 SC 564.

AIR 1967 SC 1643 overruled in AIR 1973 SC 1461.

AIR 1967 SC 1581 overruled in AIR 1974 SC 2009.

AIR 1967 SC 1581 held no longer good law in view of AIR 1974 SC 2009 in AIR 1975 SC 1187.

AIR 1967 SC 1581 held no longer good law in view of AIR 1974 SC 209 in AIR 1976 Punj. 93.

AIR 1967 SC 1419 overruled in AIR 1979 SC 1745.

AIR 1967 SC 1581 held overruled by AIR 1974 SC 2009 in AIR 1980 SC 801.

AIR 1967 SC 799 held obiter and not followed in view of AIR 1961 SC 1655 in AIR 1982 Mad. 156.

AIR 1967 SC 1335 overruled in AIR 1968 SC 765.

AIR 1967 SCI 797 partly overruled in AIR 1968 SC 327.

AIR 1967 SC 295 not approved in AIR 1969 SC 707.

AIR 1967 SC 637 overruled in AIR 1969 SC 634.

AIR 1967 SC 637 held overruled by AIR 1969 SC 634 as interpreted in AIR 1970 Cal. 15.

1968

AIR 1968 SC 1351 held not good law in view of the ealier larger Bench decision in AIR 1968 SC 466 AIR 1974 All. 337.

AIR 1968 SC 615 not followed in view of AIR 1968 SC 151 and (1969) 2SCR 60 in AIR 1977 Del. 209.

AIR 1968 SC 1053 held no good law in view of AIR 1970 SC 564 in AIR 1978 SC 803.

AIR 1968 SC 554 overruled in AIR 1978 SC 548. 1968 (40) FLR 309 SC overruled in AIR 1985 SC 89.

1968 (70) ITR 89 (SC) held no longer good law in view of Cr. P.C. 1974 in AIR 1988 SC 2267.

AIR 1968 SC 133 not approved in AIR 1989 SC 1988.

1969

AIR 1969 SC 147 dissented-distinguished in AIR 1969 Ker. 205.

AIR 1969 NSC 186 not followed in AIR 1974 SC 1596.

AIR 1969 SC 1335 overruled in AIR 1977 SC 282.

AIR 1969 SC 276 overruled in AIR 1978 SC 548.

AIR 1969 SC 1273 overruled in AIR 1980 SC 1708.

1970

Ser.L.R. 768 overruled in AIR 1974 SC 1631.

AIR 1970 SC 93 overruled in AIR 2006 SC 212(D).

AIR 1970 SC 1244 overruled in AIR 1975 SC 1331.

AIR 1970 SC 1475 not followed in view of AIR 1966 SC 806 in AIR 1976 Kar. 153.

AIR 1970 SC 1446 dissented in AIR 1977 SC 1361.

AIR 1970 SC 406 held no longer good law in view of Amdt. of 1976 in AIR 1978 Ori. 179.

AIR 1970 SC 1407 overruled in AIR 1978 SC 548.

AIR 1970 SC 406 not good law in view of AIR 1986 Del. 286.

AIR 1970 SC 852 held not good law in view of Introduction of S. 5A of COFEPOSA Act in AIR 1987 SC 1748.

AIR 1970 SC 1656 held no longer good law in view of Amdt. of T.N. Act 18 of 1960 in 1973, in AIR 1990 SC 2289.

AIR 1970 SC 406 held no loger good law in view of Amdt. in S. 115 CPC by 1976 Act in AIR 1993 Pat. 122.

AIR 1970 SC 2000 not good law in view of AIR 1978 SC 449 and AIR 1979 SC 1158 in AIR 1997 SC 1252.

AIR 1970 SC 732 overruled in AIR 2002 SC 1895.

AIR 1970 SC 77 held per incuriam in AIR 2006 SC 2511 (D).

1971

AIR 1971 SC 823 overruled in AIR 1972 SC 554.

AIR 1971 SC 1547 overruled in AIR 1974 SC 2192.

AIR 1971 SC 1828 overruled in AIR 1975 SC 1331.

AIR 1971 SC 2277 held no longer good law in view of AIR 1975 SC 156 in AIR 1977 SC 247.

AIR 1971 SC 1708 overruled in AIR 1979 SC 437.

AIR 1971 SC 1667 held no longer good law in view of new Cr.RC. (1974) in AIR 1981 SC 2198.

AIR 1971 SC 2486 held no longer good law in view of new Cr. R.C. (1974) in AIR 1981 SC 2198.

AIR 1971 SC 1828 not followed in AIR 1989 SC 341.

1971 (3) SCC 821 overruled in AIR 1995 SC 724.

AIR 1971 SC 2533 overruled in AIR 2001 SC 393.

AIR 1971 SC 330 overruled in AIR 2005 SC 688.

1972

AIR 1972 SC 1546 overruled in AIR 1974 SC 1631.

AIR 1972 SC 1640 overruled in AIR 1974 SC 1631.

AIR 1972 SC 1487 no longer good law in AIR 1975 SC 1116.

AIR 1972 SC 2526 not followed in view of AIR 1976 SC 2229 in AIR 1982 AP 227.

AIR 1972 SC 121 no longer good law in view of Amdt. in AIR 1985 SC 1683.

1972 Tax. L.R. 1011 (SC) held obiter in AIR 1991 SC 2278.

AIR 1972 SC 2526 overruled in AIR 1976 SC 2229 as stated in AIR 2003 SC 229.

AIR 1972 SC 1840 overruled in AIR 2005 SP 800.

1973

AIR 1973 SC 2761 overruled in AIR 1975 SC 1996.

AIR 1973 SC 2110 overruled in AIR 1976 SC 2358.

AIR 1973 SC 668 partly overruled AIR l978 SC 449.

AIR 1973 SC 947 not followed in AIR 1982 SC 1325.

AIR 1973 SC 2451 not followed in view of AIR 1980 SC 2051 in AIR 1982 Pat. 235.

AIR 1973 SC 930 overruled in AIR 1993 SC 477.

AIR 1973 SC 2418 overruled in AIR 1999 SC 2181.

1974

CA 1759/1969 dt. 17.5.1974 (SC) overruled in AIR 1974 SC 1940.

AIR 1974 SC 1161 overruled in AIR 1974 SC 2154.

AIR 1974 SC 1218 overruled in AIR 1975 SC 43.

AIR 1974 SC 2061 overruled in AIR 1979 SC 1745.

AIR 1974 SC 1265 impliedly overruled in AIR 1984 SC 29.

1975

AIR 1975 SC 308 held no longer good law in view of legislative changes in AIR 1975 SC 2299.

AIR 1975 SC 189 overruled in AIR 1978 SC 933.

AIR 1975 SC 2032 overruled in AIR 1978 SC 548.

AIR 1975 SC 1111 overruled in AIR 1979 SC 1745.

AIR 1975 SC 1146 not followed in view of AIR 1954 SC 728 and AIR 1964 SC 925 in AIR 1982 SC 1325.

AIR 1975 SC 1146 dissented in AIR 1983 SC 1155.

AIR 1975 SC 2216 overruled in AIR 1985 SC 1416.

(1975) 1 SCR 483 overruled in AIR 1986 SC 319.

1976

AIR 1976 SC 588 not 5 followed in view of AIR 1976 SC 869 in AIR 1977 NOC 136A (HP).

AIR 1976 SC 2198 overruled in AIR 1977 SC 1944.

AIR 1976 SC 203 overruled in AIR 1979 SC 1960.

AIR 1976 SC 588 overruled in AIR 1979 SC 1745.

AIR 1976 SC 10 partly overruled in AIR 1980 SC 387.

AIR 1976 SC 348 overruled in AIR 1980 SC 387.

AIR 1976 SC 1988 held per incuriam in AIR 1985 SC 1635.

AIR 1976 SC 2433 not followed in view of AIR 1977 SC 2319 in AIR 1988 Cal. 1.

AIR 1976 SC 1207, overruled in AIR 2017 SC 4161 (A)

1977

AIR 1977 SC 1285 held not good law in AIR 1979 SC 798.

AIR 1977 SC 2129 overruled in AIR 1979 SC 1960.

AIR 1977 SC 1361 held no longer good law in view of the 44th Constitutional Amdt. in AIR 1982 SC 710.

AIR 1977 SC 1986 overruled by AIR 1980 SC 587 in AIR 1984 SC 1392.

AIR 1977 SC 687 held per incuriam AIR 1985 SC 1293.

AIR 1977 SC 687 overruled AIR 1985 SC 1293

AIR 1977 SC 1459 overruled in AIR 1986 SC 649.

AIR 1977 SC 1555 not followed in view of AIR

1987 SC 203 in AIR 1989 Ker. 171.

AIR 1977 SC 1361 dissented in AIR 1994 SC 1918.

1978

AIR 1978 SC 955 overruled in AIR 1985 SC 796.

AIR 1978 SC 1283 reversed in AIR 1989 SC 1764.

AIR 1978 SC 995 overruled in AIR 2002 SC 643.

1979

AIR 1979 SC 336 overruled in AIR 1980 SC 57.

AIR 1979 SC 621 dissented in AIR 1980 SC 1285.

AIR 1979 SC 916 overruled in AIR 1980 SC 898.

AIR 1979 SC 964 overruled in AIR 1980 SC 898.

AIR 1979 SC 1691 overruled in AIR 1985 SC 1585.

AIR 1979 SC 362 overruled in AIR 1985 SC 943.

AIR 1979 SC 1953 held per incuriam in AIR 1988 SC 2090.

AIR 1979 SC 765 held obiter in AIR 1988 SC 481.

AIR 1979 SC 1034 overruled in AIR 1990 SC 857.

AIR 1979 SC 1501 overruled in AIR 1991 SC 574.

AIR 1979 SC 1191 held no good law in view of AIR 1971 SC 2355 in AIR 1991 SC 993.

W.P. No. 845 of 1979 dt. 15.10.1979 (SC) overmled in AIR 1991 SC 574.

AIR 1979 SC 984 overruled in AIR 2001 SC 1968.

1980

AIR 1980 SC 635 not followed in view of 1980 All L.J. 651 (SC) in AIR 1981 All. 300.

AIR 1980 SC 1118 distinguished/not followed in AIR 1981 Punj. 213.

AIR 1980 SC 1682 overruled in AIR 1983 SC 239.

AIR 1980 SC 953 overruled in AIR 1987 SC 1907.

(1980) 4 SCC 556 no longer good law in view of AIR 1980 SC 1522 in AIR 1996 SC 942.

AIR 1980 SC 1227 overruled in AIR 1999 SC 3496.

AIR 1980 SC 1955 does not stand overruled by AIR 1990 SC 1947 as stated in AIR 2003 SC 3436.

AIR 1980 SC 150 overruled in AIR 2006 SC 3446.

1981

AIR 1981 SC 1106 overruled in AIR 1986 SC 293.

(1981) 2 SCC 420 held per incuriam in AIR 1988 SC 2090.

AIR 1981 SC 2005 doubted in AIR 1989 SC 1529.

AIR 1981 SC 1887 overruled in AIR 1994 SC 1393.

AIR 1981 SC 2045 overruled in AIR 1999 SC 2894.

AIR 1981 SC 547 overruled in AIR 2005 SC 688.

AIR 1981 SC 1220 not good law in view of Crl.P.C. Amdt. Act 45 of 1978 in AIR 2003 SC 4187.

AIR 1981 SC 2075 overruled in AIR 2018 SC 1

1982

AIR 1982 SC 1439 overruled in AIR 1985 SC 1050.

AIR 1982 SC 685 doubted in AIR 1989 SC 1529.

AIR 1982 SC 149 overruled in AIR 1994 SC 268.

AIR 1982 SC 1500 overruled in AIR 1997 SC 1554.

AIR 1982 SC 1064 not followed in AIR 2001 SC 1210.

AIR 1982 SC 1569, overruled in AIR 2014 SC 1290.

1983

AIR 1983 SC 361 overruled in AIR 1983 SC 465.

AIR 1983 SC 361 overruled in AIR 1989 SC 142 and in AIR 1989 SC 1335.

1984

AIR 1984 SC 503 not followed in view of AIR 1977 SC 2147 in AIR 1987 Pat. 274.

AIR 1984 SC 186 held obiter in AIR 1988 SC 481.

AIR 1984 SC 790 held no longer good law in view of AIR 1986 SC 412 and AIR 1980 SC 614 overruled in AIR 1990 SC 1927.

AIR 1984 SC 866 partly overruled in AIR 1994 SC 2319.

AIR 1984 SC 1796 dissented in AIR 2001 SC 2255.

AIR 1984 SC 1824 overruled in AIR 2012 SC 2795

AIR 1984 SC 790, overruled in AIR 2016 SC 3469 (A)

1985

AIR 1985 SC 576 overruled in AIR 1985 SC 1576.

AIR 1985 SC 817 held obiter in AIR 1993 SC 477.

AIR 1985 SC 1118 overruled in AIR 1995 SC 676.

1985 (2) SCC 644 overruled in AIR 1995 SC 1457.

AIR 1985 SC 413 overruled in AIR 1996 SC 3128.

1985 Supp. SCC 476 overruled in AIR 2002 SC 452.

AIR 1985 SC 814 not good law in view of AIR 1987 SC 1073 in AIR 2003 SC 724.

1986

Nil

1987

AIR 1987 SC 2001 overruled in AIR 1988 SC 584.

(1987) 5 JT 472 (SC) held per incuriam in AIR 1988 SC 648.

AIR 1987 SC 1748 doubted in AIR 1989 SC 1529.

AIR 1987 SC 1383 doubted in AIR 1989 SC 1529.

AIR 1987 SC 758 overruled in AIR 1989 SC 1933.

AIR 1987 SC 53 overruled in AIR 1990 SC 933.

AIR 1987 SC 68 overruled in AIR 1992 SC 207.

AIR 1987 SC 948 not followed in view of AIR 1980 SC 563 and AIR 1971 SC 40 in AIR 1992 SC 1020.

AIR 1987 SC 1078 overruled in AIR 1992 SC 1740.

AIR 1987 SC 1500 overruled in AIR 1996 SC 2439.

1987 Supp. SCC 200 overruled in AIR 2000 SC 1822.

1987 Supp. SCC 254 overruled in AIR 2000 SC 1822.

AIR 1987 SC 242 overruled in AIR 2003 SC 1863.

1988

AIR 1988 SC 719 held per incuriam in AIR 1989 Pat 183.

1988 (Supp.) SCC 568 overruled in AIR 1990 SC 1086.

C.A. 4445/1988 dt. 1.6.12.1988 (SC) overruled in AIR 1992 SC 696.

AIR 1988 SC 1531 held to be obiter in AIR 1992 SC 248.

AIR 1988 SC 1520 overruled in AIR 1992 SC 732.

AIR 1988 SC 959 not good law in view of AIR 1974 SC 1389, AIR 1984 SC 1420 in AIR 1997 SC 2487.

AIR 1988 SC 2111 overruled in AIR 1999 SC 2181.

AIR 1988 SC 1172 not followed in view of (1997) 9 SCC 97 in AIR 2001 Del. 82.

AIR 1988 SC 1520 overruled in AIR 2001 SC 626.

(1988)38 ELR212(SC) overruled in AIR 2001 SC 393.

1989

AIR 1989 SC 2218 not followed in view of AIR 1980 SC 563 and AIR 1971 SC 40 in AIR 1992 SC 1020.

1989 Supp. (2) SCR 140 overruled in AIR 1994 SC 526.

AIR 1989 SC 1247 overruled in AIR 1996 SC 238.

AIR 1989 SC 644 dissented in AIR 1996 SC 524.

1989 Supp. (2) SCC 655 overruled in AIR 2000 SC 1822.

AIR 1989 SC 2060 overruled in AIR 2002 SC 77.

AIR 1989 SC 1456 not good law in view of the Crl.P.C. Amdt. Act 45 of 1978 in AIR 2003 SC 4187.

AIR 1989 SC 1160 overruled in AIR 2003 SC 3854.

1990

1990 All.W.C. 308 (SC) not followed in view of AIR 1980 SC 892 and AIR 1980 SC 1575 in AIR 1991 All. 114.

AIR 1990 SC 781 overruled in AIR 1993 SC 1048.

AIR 1990 SC 71 overruled in AlR 1993 SC l.

AIR 1990 SC 1923 overruled in AIR 1994 SC 1484.

AIR 1990 SC 781 overruled in AIR 1994 SC 2291.

1990 Supp. SCC 640 overruled in AIR 1994 SC 1884.

1990 Supp. SCC 350 overruled in AIR 1994 SC 1884.

1990 Supp. SCC 350 overruled in AIR 1995 SC 1457.

AIR 1990 SC 937 overruled in AIR 1996 SC 2890.

AIR 1990 SC 2174 overruled in AIR 1997 SC 2661.

AIR 1990 SC 933 overruled in AIR 2001 SC 2699.

1990 (4) SCC 178 overruled in AIR 2003 SC 4603.

1991

1991 AIR SCW 3026 overruled in AIR 1997 SC 645.

1991 AIR SCW 2391 overruled in AIR 2001 SC 1133.

AIR 1991 SC 1134 overruled in AIR 2003 SC 4506.

AIR 1991 SC 259 overruled in AIR 2003 SC 3854.

1992

1992 AIR SCW 2100 partly overruled in AIR 1993 SC 2178.

1992 (1) SCC 673 overruled in AIR 1995 SC in 1012.

1992 AIR SCW 1305 overruled in AIR 1999 SC 468.

1992 AIR SCW 3639 overruled in AIR 2002 SC 834.

AIR 1992 SC 732 Disting AIR 2015 SC 2749.

1993

1993 AIR SCW 2198 overruled in AIR 1995 SC 372.

1993 AIR SCW 771 overruled in AIR 1998 SC 3148.

AIR 1993 SC 787 overruled in AIR 2000 SC 1717.

1993 AIR SCW 2740 overruled in AIR 2002 SC 5.

AIR 1993 SC 2178 overruled in AIR 2003 SC 355.

1994

1994 AIR SCW 1764 overruled in AIR 1996 SC 946.

AIR 1994 SC 1591 not followed in view of AIR 1985 SC 1416 and AIR 1966 SC 948 in AIR 1996 Kar. 274.

AIR 1994 SC 923 overruled in AIR 1996 SC 1643.

1994 AIR SCW 2901 overruled in AIR 1998 SC 2713.

1994 AIR SCW 2515 overruled in AIR 1999 SC 2894.

1994 AIR SCW 1552 overruled in AIR 2001 SC 1117.

1994 AIR SCW 2181 held per incuriam in AIR 2004 SC 754.

1994 AIR SCW 2210 overruled in AIR 2006 SC 951(E).

1994 Supp. (3)SCC 126 held per incuriam in AIR 2006 Raj. 237.

(1994) 2 SCC 445 overruled in AIR 2003 SC 1191.

1995

1995 AIR SCW 65 overruled in AIR 1995 SC 2259.

1995 (1) Scale 21 (SC) overruled in AIR 1995 SC 2259.

1995 AIR SCW 2942 partly overruled in AIR 1997 SC 645.

1995 AIR SCW 3488 overruled in AIR 1998 SC 1895.

1995 Supp. (1) SCC 432 overruled in AIR 1998 SC 1767.

1995 AIR SCW 901 overruled in AIR 2000 SC 860.

1995 AIR SCW 2139 overruled in AIR 2000 SC 197.

1995 AIR SCW 871 overruled in AIR 2001 SC 117.

1995 AIR SCW 3668 overruled in AIR 2001 SC 2951.

1995 AIR SCW 3817 overruled in AIR 2001 SC 2951.

1995 Supp. (1) SCC 673 overruled in AIR 2006 SC 2550(D)

1995 AIR SCW 4140 overruled in AIR 2002 SC 3372.

AIR 1995 SC 1681, overruled in AIR 2016 SC 1213.

1996

1996 AIR SCW 864 overruled in AIR 2006 SC 2550(D).

1996 AIR SCW 1365 overruled in AIR 1998 SC 656.

1996 AIR SCW 1015 overruled in AIR 1998 SC 2086.

1996 AIR SCW 840 overrulcd in AIR 1998 SC 1057.

(1996) 6 SCC 369 overruled in AIR 1998 SC 1057.

1996 AIR SCW 3696 reversed in AIR 1999 SC 2979.

AIR 1996 SC 977 not good law in view of AIR 1974 SC 348 in AIR 1999 SC 378.

C.A. No. 1690/1996 dated 6.11.1996 (SC) overruled in AIR 1999 SC 3502.

1996 AIR SCW 1493 not good law in AIR 2000 SC 2587.

1996 AIR SCW 2498 overruled in AIR 2006 SC 212(D)

1996 AIR SCW 2672 overruled in AIR 2001 SC 2472.

1996 AIR SCW 2715 not good law in view of 1999 AIR SCW 1156 in AIR 2001 SC 3924.

1996 AIR SCW 2776 overruled in AIR 2001 SC 2472.

1996 AIR SCW 3189 overruled in AIR 2001 SC 3134.

(1996) 2 SCC 541 overruled in AIR 2001 SC 3332.

1996 AIR SCW 2297 overruled in AIR 2002 SC 1856.

1996 (3) SCC 88 overruled in AIR 2002 SC 1334.

(1996) NSCC 619 overruled in AIR 2002 SC 1334.

AIR 1996 SC 3516 overruled in AIR 2003 SC 2000.

AIR 1996 SC 2073 impliedly overruled in AIR 2003 SC 1563.

AIR 1996 SC 1691 not good law in view of AIR 1998 SC 2939 in AIR 2003 SC 51

1996 Pat. L.R. 110 (SC) overruled in AIR 2003 SC 1637.

AIR 1996 SC 1308 overruled in AIR 2005 SC 614.

AIR 1996 SC 223 not good law in view of AIR 1964 SC 1320 in AIR 2005 SC 622.

1996 (6) SCC 766 overruled in AIR 2005 SC 359.

1996 AIR SCW 2005 overruled in AIR 2006 SC 1908 (A).

1996 AIR SCW 864 overruled in AIR 2006 SC 2550.

AIR 1996 SC 1042 held per incuriam in AIR 2011 SC 312.

1996 AIR SCW 1548 overruled in 2001 AIR SCW 1689-AIR 2008 SC (Supp.) 337.

AIR 1996 SC 2853 not good law in AIR 2009 SC (Supp.) 2032-AIR 2011 SC 2620.

AIR 1996 SC 1340, overruled in AIR 2014 SC 1400(E)

AIR 1996 SC 1182 Held per incuriam AIR 2015 SC 1402

1996 (4) SCC 148 overruled in AIR 2016 SC 3340

AIR 1996 SC 765 overruled in AIR 2016 SC 4107

AIR 1996 SC 1627 Held per incuriam - AIR 2017 SC 4609 (A)

AIR 1996 SC 196 Not followed since it was held as Not Good Law in 2009 AIR SCW 5536.

1997

1997 AIR SCW 424 overruled in AIR 1997 SC 3801.

1997 AIR SCW 3113 overruled in AIR 1998 SC 1767.

AIR 1997 SC 2817 overruled in AIR 1998 SC 656.

1997 AIR SCW 2426 overruled in AIR 1998 SC 1769.

1997 AIR SCW 1937 overruled in AIR 1998 SC 1767.

1997 AIR SCW 106 overruled in AIR 1998 SC 815.

1997 AIR SCW 4166 dissented in AIR 1999 SC 2640.

1997 AIR SCW 3574 overruled in AIR 1999 SC 2460.

1997 AIR SCW 2274 overruled in AIR 1999 SC 2894.

1997 AIR SCW 2257 overruled in AIR 1999 SC 3471.

1997 AIR SCW 1636 reversed in AIR 1999 SC 2979.

(1997) 5 SCC 430 not followed in view of AIR 1997 SC 2564 in AIR 1999 SC 3822.

1997 (6) SCC 78 not good law AIR 2000 SC 2587.

1997 (8) JT SC 528 overruled in AIR 2000 SC 1724.

1997 AIR SCW 430 overruled in AIR 2001 SC 3527.

1997 AIR SCW 3331 overruled in AIR 2001 SC 3234.

1997 AIR SCW 4166 held not good law in view of 1999 AIR SCW 1899 in AIR 2002 SC 2241.

AIR 1997 SC 3072 overruled in AIR 2003 SC 320.

AIR 1997 SC 1208 not good law in view of C.A.No.4355/1985 dt. 30.2.2002 in AIR 2003 SC 4650.

1997 AIR SCW 3348 not good law in AIR 2009 SC (Supp.) 780.

1997 AIR SCW 274 overruled in 1998 AIR SCW 1553-AIR 2010 SC 1851.

AIR 1997 SC 1788 Not good law - AIR 2016 SC 5176 (B)

AIR 1997 SC 1511 overruled in AIR 2017 SC 4609 (A)

AIR 1997 SC 3614, Held not good law in view of AIR 1963 SC 996 - AIR 2017 SC 4609(D)

AIR 1997 SC 2658 overruled in AIR 2018 SC 3606 (A).

1998

1998 AIR SCW 965 overruled in AIR 1998 SC 2713.

1998 AIR SCW 319 overruled in AIR 2000 SC 1102.

1998 AIR SCW 3928 overruled in AIR 2000 SC 1102.

1998 AIR SCW 3208 overruled in AIR 2002 SC 1856.

1998 (9) SCC 138 held per incuriam in AIR 2002 SC 1598.

1998 (9) SCC 348 held per incuriam AIR 2011 SC 312.

AIR 1998 SC 142 overruled in 2006 AIR SCW 4791 and AIR 2013 SC 217.

AIR 1998 SC 3148 overruled in AIR 2013 SC 3018.

1998 (9) SCC 706 held per incuriam AIR 2015 SC 901.

AIR 1998 SC 1251 overruled in AIR 2016 SC 3340.

1999

1999 (9) JT 308 (SC) overruled in AIR 2000 SC 402.

1999 AIR SCW 3440 overruled in AIR 2002 SC 2973.

1999 AIR SCW 3522 overruled in AIR 2002 SC 1856.

AIR 1999 SC 3455 not good law in view of AIR 2002 SC 2973 in AIR 2003 SC 209.

AIR 1999 SC 2626 held per incuriam in AIR 2003 SC 4317.

AIR 1999 SC 1837 held per incuriam in AIR 2003 SC 3534.

AIR 1999 SC 1747 overruled in AIR 2003 SC 1555.

AIR 1999 SC 495 over-ruled in AIR 2003 SC 646.

1999 SCC (Crl.) 371 overruled in AIR 2004 SC 1990: 2008 AIR SCW 2119-AIR 2011 SC 1748.

AIR 1999 SC 1609 overruled in AIR 2013 SC 3283.

AIR 1999 SC 3762 overruled in AIR 2014 SC 3519.

2000

(2000) 8 JT (SC) 248 overruled in AIR 2005 SC 3187.

2000 AIR SCW 2172 overruled in AIR 2001 SC 1952.

2000 AIR SCW 722 overruled in AIR 2001 SC 2763.

2000 AIR SCW 1561 overruled in AIR 2002 SC 77.

2000 (9) JT (SC) 32 overruled in AIR 2002 SC 3687.

W. P. Crl. 72/2000 dt. 5. 5. 2000 SC overruled in AIR 2002 SC 3687.

AIR 2000 SC 2264 overruled in AIR 2006 SC 2731.

AIR 2000 SC 3751 held per incuriam in AIR 2011 SC 1989.

AIR 2000 SC 197 no longer good law in AIR 2003 SC 843.

AIR 2000 SC 235 overruled in AIR 2003 SC 607.

2000 AIR SCW 3908 overruled in AIR 2006 SC 450(A).

2000 Cr.LJ 3485 (SC) not good law in 1999 Cr.LJ 3672 (SC)-AIR 2011 SC 77.

AIR 2000 SC 1565 overruled in AIR 2012 SC 86.

AIR 2000 SC 145 partly overruled in AIR 2012 SC 2795

Observation to contrary in AIR 2000 SC 1535, Not good law - AIR 2013 SC 2036.

AIR 2000 SC 3243 overruled - AIR 2014 SC 142.

AIR 2000 SC 1073, partly overruled in AIR 2014 SC 1446.

AIR 2000 SC 808, No longer good law in AIR 2001 SC 862,- AIR 2015 SC 1098.

AIR 2000 SC 2946 overruled-AIR 2015 SC 157.

2001

AIR 2001 SC 649 overruled in AIR 2003 SC 3157.

2001 Cr.LJ 128 (SC) not good law in view of 1990 Cr.LJ. 1599 (SC); AIR 2007 (NOC) 2041 (Ker.).

2001 Cr.LJ 2346 (SC) not good law in view of 1990 Cr.LJ. 1599 (SC); AIR 2007 (NOC) 2041 (Ker.).

2001 AIR SCW 134, overruled in AIR 2010 SC 188.

2001 AIR SCW 2307, overruled - AIR 2014 SC 3057.

AIR 2001 SC 1273 overruled in AIR 2016 SC 1213 (C).

AIR 2001 SC 2856 overruled in AIR 2018 SC 2039 (B).

2002

AIR 2002 SCW 273 overruled in AIR 2002 SC 3350.

2002 AIR SCW 3575 overruled in AIR 2002 SC 1045.

AIR 2002 SC 3629 held per incuriam in AIR 2002 SC 551.

AIR 2002 SC 2445 overruled in AIR 2016 SC 1213(E).

2003

2003 AIR SCW 5844 overruled in AIR 2007 SC 950.

2003 AIR SCW 695 overruled in AIR 2006 SC 1138 (D).

AIR 2003 SC 4453 overruled - AIR 2014 SC 2895.

2004

2004 AIR 533 (SC) held per incuriam in AIR 2008 SC 845.

AIR 2004 SC 3751 held per incuriam in AIR 2011 SC 1989.

AIR 2004 SC 486 not good law in 1999 Cr.LJ 3672 (SC) -AIR 2011 SC 77.

AIR 2004 SC 1890 held per incuriam in AIR 2012 SC 1485.

AIR 2004 SC 536 held per incuriam in AIR 2012 SC 1485.

AIR 2004 SC 834 dissented from AIR 2013 SC 666.

AIR 2004 SC 4776 Impliedly overruled in AIR 2018 SC 2670.

2005

AIR 2005 SC 1057 held per incuriam in AIR 2011 SC 312.

AIR 2005 SC 498 held per incuriam in AIR 2011 SC 312.

AIR 2005 SC 2994 held per incuriam in AIR 2011 SC 1989.

AIR 2005 SC 4284 Disting -AIR 2015 SC 2757.

AIR 2005 SC 3820 overruled AIR 2015 SC 180.

AIR 2005 SC 2132 overruled in AIR 2016 SC 3340.

2006

2006 AIR SCW 3865 held per incuriam in AIR 2007 SC 528.

2006 AIR SCW 3865 held per incuriam in AIR 2007 SC 893.

AIR 2006 SC 2571 overruled in AIR 2013 SC 2714.

AIR 2006 SC 2511 overruled - AIR 2013 SC 2741.

2006 AIR SCW 5666, overruled - AIR 2014 SC 3625.

AIR 2006 SC 1806, Disting - AIR 2015 SC 3473.

AIR 2006 SC 2550 overruled AIR 2016 SC 5617 (A).

2007

2007 AIR SCW 4323 overruled in AIR 2009 SC (Supp.) 780.

2007 (9) SCC 665 overruled in AIR 2009 (Supp.) 780.

AIR 2007 SC (Supp.) 1280: 2007 AIR SCW 4323 not good law in view of AIR 2010 SC 1881.

AIR 2007 SC 1208 held per incuriam in AIR 2012 SC 3144.

AIR 2007 SC 1899, overruled in AIR 2014 SC 1400 (L).

AIR 2007 SC 763 overruled in AIR 2015 SC 1359.

2008

2008 AIR SCW 406 dissented from AIR 2008 SC 2116.

AIR 2008 SC (Supp.) 668 overruled in AIR 2009 SC (Supp.) 780.

AIR 2008 SC 218 held per incuriam in AIR 2011 SC312.

AIR 2008 SC 693 overruled in AIR 2011 SC 1175.

AIR 2008 SC 218 Held per incuriam-AIR 2011 SC 312.

AIR 2008 SC (Supp) 1 overruled in AIR 2014 SC 2114 (B).

AIR 2008 SC (Supp) 1887 held per incuriam - AIR 2015 SC 2275.

AIR 2008 SC 2266 overruled in AIR 2017 SC 3668 (A).

AIR 2008 SC 1418, Partly overruled in AIR 2017 SC 3668 (A).

2009

AIR 2009 SC 1114 overruled in AIR 2013 SC 2741.

AIR 2009 SC 2387 held per incuriam - AIR 2011 SC 1748.

AIR 2009 SC 3127 overruled-AIR 2011 SC 3495.

AIR 2009 SC (Supp.) 1619 held per incuriam in AIR 2012 SC 3144.

AIR 2009 SC (Supp) 1619 Held per incuriam - AIR 2012 SC 3144.

AIR 2009 SC 1114, overruled - AIR 2013 SC 2714.

2009 - Spl. Civil Appln. No. 18692 of 2005, D/- 26-6-2009, Reversed in AIR 2015 SC 2348.

2009 AIR SCW 1614, held not good law - AIR 2015 SC 254.

AIR 2009 SC 2151, overruled in AIR 2017 SC 3668 (A).

2010

AIR 2010 SC 383 not good law in AIR 2009 SC (Supp.) 2032-AIR 2011 SC 2620.

(2010) 10 SCC 225 overruled in AIR 2012 SC 1266.

2010 AIR SCW 331, Not good law - AIR 2014 SC 3723

AIR 2010 SC 1511 overruled AIR 2015 SC 856.

2011

2011 (14) SCC 758, Impliedly overruled in AIR 2014 SC 1393.

AIR 2011 SC (Supp) 755, Not a good law-AIR 2014 SC 3036

2012

2012 (6) SCC 102, Partly overruled in AIR 2014 SC 2114 (F).

AIR 2012 SC 1751, Disting - AIR 2015 SC 3469.

AIR 2012 SC 3016, overruled - AIR 2017 SC 3271 (C).

AIR 2012 SC 2351, overruled in AIR 2017 SC 4609 (A).

2013

2013 AIR SCW 5477 overruled in AIR 2014 SC 3519.

AIR 2013 SC (Cri) 1034 overruled in AIR 2015 SC 1359.

AIR 2013 SC 2248 overruled in AIR 2016 SC 4245.

AIR 2013 SC 2924 Held per incuriam - AIR 2017 SC 2141.

2013 (16) SCC 526 overruled in AIR 2017 SC 3271 (C).

2013 (9) SCC 54, overruled in AIR 2017 SC 5157 (A).

2014

2014 (2) SCC 266 overruled - AIR 2014 SC 3519.

2014 (5) Scale 641 overruled in AIR 2015 SC 1359.

AIR 2014 SC 2242 impliedly overruled in AIR 2018 SC 824 (C) 2014 (6) SCC 564 overruled in AIR 2018 SC

824 (H).

2015

2015 (3) Scale 34 overruled in AIR 2015 SC 2006

AIR 2015 SC 706. Held, No longer good law in view of CPC Amendment of 1976.

2015 (3) SCC 353 overruled in AIR 2018 SC 824 (C).

AIR 2015 SC 2041 Impliedly overruled in AIR 2018 SC 824 (C).

2015 (8) SCC 544 Impliedly overruled in AIR 2018 SC 824 (C).

AIR 2015 SC 1462 overruled in AIR 2018 SC 824 (F).

2015 (3) SCC 353 Overruled in AIR 2018 SC 824 (H).

2015 (3) SCC 206 overruled in AIR 2018 SC 824 (H).

AIR 2015 SC 710 overruled in AIR 2018 SC 1895 (A).

2016

AIR 2016 SC 33 overruled in AIR 2017 SC 4609 (A).

AIR 2016 SC 2584 Impliedly overruled in AIR 2018 SC 824 (C).

2017

AIR 2017 SC 2967 overruled in AIR 2017 SC 4609 (A).

References

1. Acharya, N.K. (revised by Dewan, V.K.)	Landmark Judgments of Supreme Court (1950–2018), Asia Law House Opp. High Court, Hyderabad-2, 5th Edition, Year 2019, Total pages 964.
2. Agrawal, Dr. P.K. & Chaturvedi, Dr. K.N.	Commentary on the Constitution of India, published by Prabhat Prakashan, 4/19 Asaf Ali Road, New Delhi-110002, Year 2017, Total Pages, 496.
3. Agrawal, Dr. P.K. Gupta, Virag	The Constitution of India (Bare Act with short notes), Prabhat Paperbacks, 4/19, Asaf Ali Road, New Delhi-110002, Year 2019, Total pages 283.
4. Antony, M.J.	Social Action Through Courts (Landmark Judgments in Public Interest Litigation), Indian Social Institute, 10 Institutional Area, Lodi Road, New Delhi-110003, year 1993, Total pages 161.
5. Singhvi, Abhishek Sarma, Satyajit	From the Trenches, Juggernaut Books, K.S. House, 118, Shahpur Jat, New Delhi-110049, Year 2020, Total pages 225.

Journals, Reporters etc.

All India Reporter (AIR)	All India Reporter Pvt. Ltd. Congress Nagar, Nagpur-440012 Phone: +91-8380005660 E-mail: helpdesk.aironline@gmail.com Website: https://www.aironline.in/air-legal-judgment.html
Supreme Court Cases (SCC)	Supreme Court Cases: The Registrar, Supreme court of India, Tilak Marg, New Delhi-110001 Ph.: 011-23388922-24, 23388942 E-mail: supremecourt@nic.in Website: https://main.sci.gov.in/publication